KID-POWERED GRAPHICS

David Fiday received his Masters degree from Northern Illinois University in Instructional Technology. He has always believed in machines as a way to individualize and humanize the education of children.

He has worked for the past three years to bring students and teachers a specific level of computer literacy. In the past two years, he and his students have logged over 50,000 computing hours on their 13 Apple II computers.

His articles have appeared in *The Computing Teacher*, *Educational Computer Magazine*, *Gifted Childrens Newsletter* and others. He is also a contributing editor to *Electronic Learning*.

He is presently at work on a Logo book for Howard W. Sams & Co., Inc. Future projects include a book for programming literacy for teachers and a children's book on the Apple IIe.

He resides in Joliet, Illinois with his wife and two lovely, computer literate daughters.

KID-POWERED GRAPHICS

by

David Fiday

Howard W. Sams & Co., Inc.
4300 WEST 62ND ST. INDIANAPOLIS, INDIANA 46268 USA

Edited by *Patricia Perry*
Illustrated by *John E. Hopper*
Production by *Christy Pierce*
            Kay Crostreet
            Larry Lynch

Preface

Thinking is the single most important activity which can be fostered in education. Linking this thinking process with DOING creates a dynamically individualized form of learning. With each activity, the student gains ground in confidence, thinking abilities, love of learning, and all the positive feeling we want them to experience.

Many computer languages can be beneficial. It is incumbent upon teachers to discover which language or languages are best for the children of their district. In ours, children react most favorably to programming in low-resolution graphics of Applesoft BASIC. They also use Logo. Using Applesoft BASIC and Logo is a part of an overall package of experiences which we feel will prepare them for the computer experiences of their future.

Color graphics make the otherwise invisible mental manipulation very concrete. Students can see—and feel excitement about—their picture programs.

They gain power over the computer, and use this power to generate meaningful programs. These programs become the measurable output of their thinking as their skills in problem solving grow.

They could have gained this skill-building through other languages, but Applesoft BASIC is suitable, meaningful, and resident in the Apple computer. It is not so much the medium which is important in this case, but rather the process. We aren't making programmers, we are helping children learn how to think through programming.

The students see these activities as reflective of the other activities they observe computers doing. They see computers everywhere. What could be more natural than to learn on one? They play games with computers, see them in airports and banks, and on pop machines. Some have them in their homes. Others use computers at school to help teachers, guidance counselors, deans, librarians, and administrators.

Children need three things to be computer literate.
1. They need to know a little about the history of computers.
2. They need to know how and when to use computers.
3. They need to know programming. Any of several languages would be best to use, but they need to know the strengths and weaknesses of each.

Kid-Powered Graphics is just one of a series of books designed to help bring the power of the computer under the fingertips of children. If we, together, can give them the power to see into and use computers as tools, we will prepare them for a world in which computers and their applications will be an overwhelming part of their daily life.

Let us make their first encounters with the computer the beginning of a thinking relationship with computers. When Johnny sits down in front of a computer, be sure that it isn't just for skill/drill. Children should program.

We don't need another book about Johnny—"Why Johnny can't compute!"

For the Laraway 70-C Children, Staff, Superintendent
    & Schoolboard
For the Friends and Loved ones who put me here:
Goldie, Jay and Vera
But mostly Bev
For New Found Friends:
Richard and a wonderful Sams Staff
For computing Children:
But mostly Jennifer and Jessica

Introduction for the teacher

People love programming because it puts them in control of their computer. The purpose of this book is to show you and your students the joy of "bossing your Apple around."

The greatest reward of our profession is to observe the active thinking experiences of our students.

On the outside we see smiles, hear yowls of excitement, and feel the electric enthusiasm of students operating computers. After a time, the noise settles into a quiet determination which reflects the "I know what I'm doing and I'm doing it by myself" thoughts the students are thinking.

The internal benefits are just as exciting. We know our students are solving problems through analysis. They are questioning themselves, weighing alternatives, and making decisions. We know they are synthesizing new ideas from the interaction of their old ideas and the new knowledge of computing skills to create something entirely unique.

This is the greatest joy we can give our students. They will always remember the rewarding experience of Learning by Doing.

To the students

Your teacher is going to help Mr. Graphix lead you on a journey which is exciting, challenging, and important to you as a growing person.

These activities will ask you to THINK-PLAN-WRITE- and DO. Don't hurry. Take your time and enjoy. Learn the commands that will help you "boss your Apple around." Once you have the commands firmly in your mind, they will be with you forever.

I wish you the best of luck, fun, and learning!

Contents

Getting ready for graphics
1

Welcome to the world of programming.
My name is Mr. Graphix.

I'm going to show you how to draw in color on the Apple II
computer.

Together we will take a very exciting journey.

Our trip will be fun because making something from our
imaginations is always exciting!!

To start you will need:

an Apple computer

a color monitor

a system master diskette (it comes with your Apple)

a blank diskette (one comes with your Apple or you may buy one)

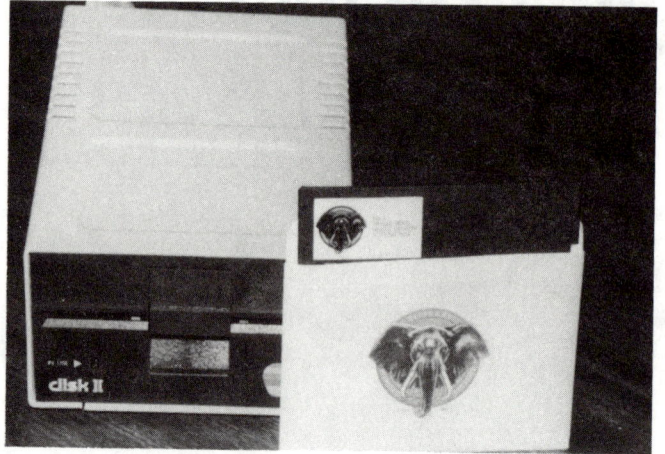

a smile and . . . . . lots of imagination!!

The graphic programs you will write are kid-powered. They get their energy and color from your mind. So rev up your imagination and let's go.

For starters, we need to agree on what certain words mean in programming. And programming is a good word to start with.

Programming means to tell the computer what to do. We are going to be bossing our Apple around. We'll tell it what to do. If we do it right, the computer will do it in a snap!

RUN PLOT

LIST GR

To program, we need a programming language. A programming language is words the computer understands. We are learning the Applesoft BASIC language.

The words in a programming language are called commands. Commands tell the computer what to do. We know what commands are. It's like at school when the teacher says, "Sit down! Take out your book! Now listen!"

Our words will tell the computer to do things, too. And since it is a good computer, like you are a good student, it will do as we say.

REMEMBER: WE MUST BE SPECIFIC. THE COMPUTER WILL DO WHAT WE TELL IT TO DO, NOT WHAT WE WANT IT TO DO.

We will be using commands over and over again. They will be as familiar as your own name very soon. If you forget what a command means, look in the index or the glossary at the back of the book. I will repeat the commands several times for you. If you do your practice reviews at the end of each chapter, you will do very well.

PROGRAMS

Programs are a series of commands with line numbers. A line number is the number which we type in front of a command. Programs need numbers so the computer knows what to do first, second, third, etc.

When we write a program, we will count by 10s: 10, 20, 30, 40, and so on.

10
20
30
40

Counting by 10s leaves unused numbers. We can use these numbers if we forget to put in a command.

EXAMPLE: Between 10 and 20, there are 9 commands—11, 12, 13, etc. THIS WILL BE VERY IMPORTANT LATER WHEN WE CHANGE OUR PROGRAMS.

For now, remember to count by 10s.

10
11
12
13
14
15
16
17
18
19
20

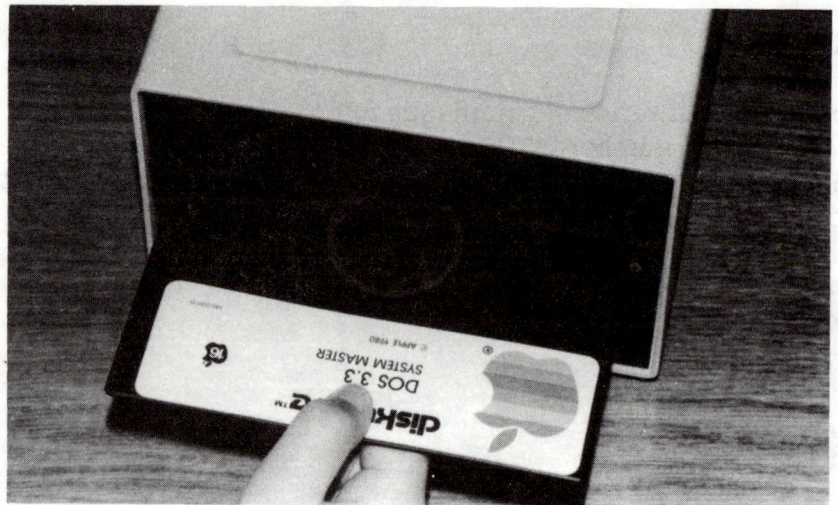

STARTING THE APPLE COMPUTER

After you have plugged in your Apple and connected the monitor or TV, open the disk drive door. Place the system master diskette into the drive. Be sure the label is up and between your thumb and index finger. Close the disk drive door.

At the left rear of the Apple is a rocker switch. Pull the top toward you. As it clicks, the disk drive will make a whirring sound. The power light on the front of the Apple and the red light on the disk drive will light up.

Turn on your monitor by turning or pulling the knob.

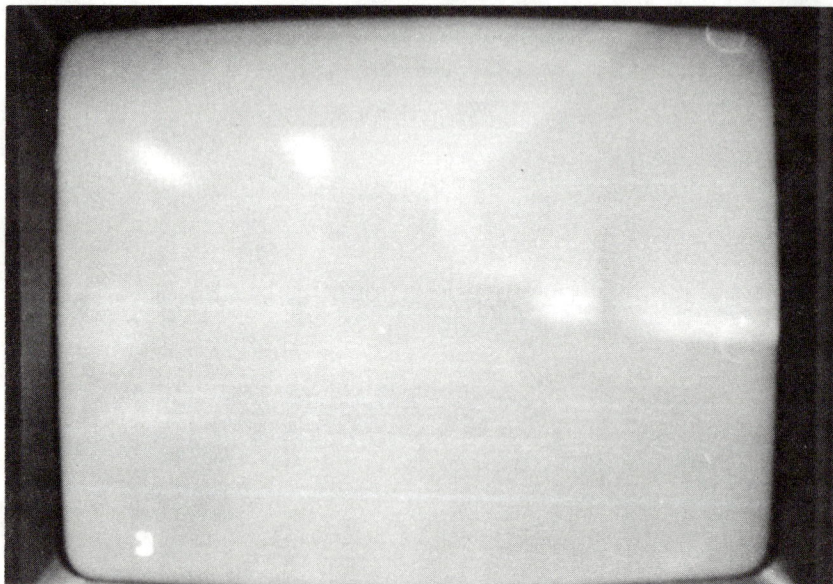

A warning about the disk drive. Never touch the disk drive door or reset key when the drive light is on.

When the red light on the disk drive goes off, a flashing white box of light should appear on the monitor. This flashing box of light is the cursor. It shows you where the next letter or number will appear. As the cursor flashes, the Apple is telling you it is waiting for you to do something.

By now, your cursor should be flashing. Since the Apple is waiting for us, let's continue.

Take out the system master diskette and put it away. Place the blank diskette into the drive with the label up and toward you.

Type the command NEW and press the return key. NEW is a command which tells the computer we have something new for its memory. The return key has the word "return" on it. It is on the right side of the keyboard.

HOW TO INITIALIZE A DISKETTE

We will now initialize the blank diskette. To do this, we must write a short program.

Type this program.
Be sure to press the return key after each line.

```
10   HOME
20   PRINT "HELLO, APPLE"
30   PRINT "I'M YOUR BOSS."
40   PRINT "I'M (Type your NAME) "
50   END
```

HOME tells the computer to clear the screen and place the cursor at the top left of the screen.

NEW is a command which tells the computer we have something new for its memory.

REMEMBER: A PROGRAM IS A SERIES OF COMMANDS WITH LINE NUMBERS.

HOME tells the computer to clear the screen and place the cursor at the top left of the screen.

PRINT tells the computer to print something on the screen. Whatever we want printed must be in quotation marks (" ").

END tells the computer there are no more commands.

LIST is a command to show the commands in number order.

PRINT tells the computer to print something on the screen. Whatever we want printed must be in quotation marks (" ")

To make quotation marks, hold down the key marked SHIFT and type the key with the quotation mark on it (the 2 key).

END tells the computer there are no more commands.

Once you have typed in your program, check to see if everything is spelled correctly. If you made a typing error, it's okay. It's easy as pie to fix.

Retype the line number and the line so it is right. Press the return key.

```
WRONG       RIGHT
10 HPME     10 HPME
            10 HOME
```

Type LIST and press the return key.

LIST is a command to show the commands in number order.

```
10   HOME
20   PRINT "HELLO, APPLE"
30   PRINT "I'M YOUR BOSS"
40   PRINT "I'M MR. GRAPHIX!"
50   END
```

The computer prints your list of commands. They are in the correct order. The computer is great for putting things in number order.

CLUNK CRUNCH CRACK SCRUNCH

If everything is typed correctly, we can continue.

Type the words INIT HELLO and press the return key.

The disk drive will make a clattering, terrible sound. Don't worry. The disk drive is working for you. While it works, read the following.

INIT is a command which makes a diskette ready to hold information.

HELLO is the name of our program.

Every time we write a program, it will have a name.

Every program must have a different name.

When we said INIT HELLO, we told the computer to save our commands under the name HELLO and to make it the first program.

We could have called our program hamburger or taco. It doesn't matter what the name is. But it must be different from the other programs on the diskette.

INIT is a command which makes a diskette ready to hold information.

"IM CALLING MY PROGRAM BOZO"

YOU'RE SUCH A CLOWN! I'M CALLING MINE CINDERELLA.

Right now, I bet your cursor is flashing again. This Apple is very impatient. It's waiting for us again.

Type the command RUN.

RUN tells the computer to do what is in its memory.

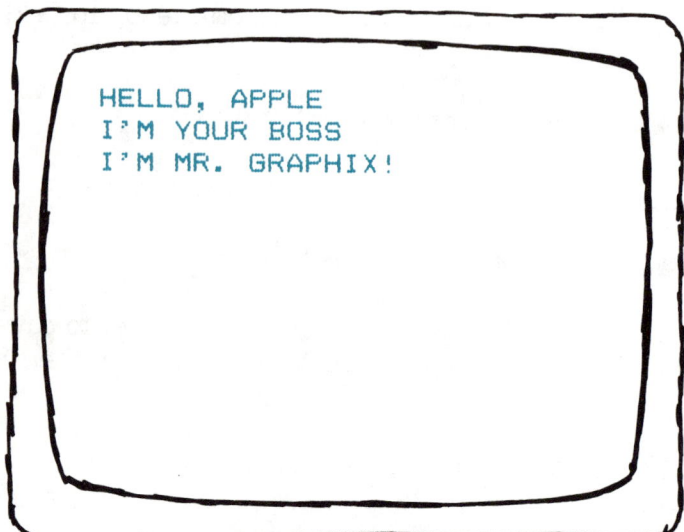

```
HELLO, APPLE
I'M YOUR BOSS
I'M MR. GRAPHIX!
```

RUN tells the computer to do what is in its memory.

There you have your first program.

Every time you run this diskette, you will remember that you are the commander of this computer.

The next time you come for a lesson, you will use this diskette to start your computer.

You want proof? Okay!

Turn off your computer. Wait five seconds.

1 2 3 4 5

Turn it on again.

Your program automatically runs to greet you.

Your program could use some space.

The sentences are *too close* to each other.

Type LIST

```
10    HOME
20    PRINT "HELLO, APPLE"
30    PRINT "I'M YOUR BOSS"
40    PRINT "I'M MR. GRAPHIX!"
```

We can practice adding lines of commands to programs.

Type the following:

```
15    PRINT
25    PRINT
35    PRINT
```

PRINT with no quotation marks (" ") or message makes the computer skip a line. It prints "nothing."

PRINT with no quotation marks (" ") or message makes the computer skip a line. It prints "nothing."

Type RUN

That's better isn't it?

We must SAVE our new program. When you change a program, you must type SAVE and the name of your program.

INIT is used to save a first program. It is used only when a blank diskette is used for the first time.

SAVE is used all the time. SAVE tells the computer to put the program on the diskette.

We will learn more about talking with the diskette in later chapters.

Do your practice review. If you want, you can create another program which prints a message. What will you say?

In Chapter 2, we will learn about the screen for low-resolution graphics. We will draw with boxes of light.

For now, I'll say—See you soon!

In review

Place the letter of the definition
in front of the word it describes.

_____ PROGRAMMING

_____ APPLESOFT BASIC

_____ COMMANDS

_____ PROGRAM

_____ LINE NUMBER

_____ CURSOR

_____ NEW

_____ HOME

_____ INIT

_____ PRINT

_____ LIST

_____ RUN

a. tells the computer to run a program.
b. tells the computer we have something new
   for its memory.
c. a flashing box of light that tells us the
   computer is waiting for its next command.
d. words that tell the computer what to do.
e. tells the computer to clear the screen and
   put cursor at top left of screen.
f. tells the computer to make a listing of the
   commands in a program.
g. tells the computer to print something on
   the screen.
h. the language we speak to our Apple.
i. the number that goes with a command in a
   program.
j. a series of commands with line numbers
   that tells the computer what to do.
k. telling the computer what to do (bossing
   around the Apple).
l. tells the computer to initialize a diskette.

GRAPHIX GRADE BOX

# CORRECT	
9–12	
6–8	
0–5	

READ THIS CHAPTER AGAIN

Plots on the screen 2

Welcome back! I missed you. You must be ready because you are here. Let's start.

The Apple computer can make colored lights appear on the screen. If we know the commands, we can make beautiful or scary pictures.

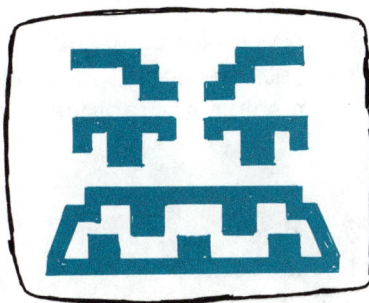

The commands are GR and COLOR=

GR tells the computer we are ready to draw in color.

COLOR= tells the computer what color we want to draw with.

Use the diskette we initialized in Chapter 1 to start the computer.

Type GR and press the return key. (I'll use *R to mean press the return key from now on. Later, when you're used to pressing the return key, I'll stop giving you the hint.)

GR tells the computer we are ready to draw in color.

COLOR= tells the computer what color we want to draw with.

After you typed GR and *R, you noticed the screen changed. The cursor is now very close to the bottom of the screen. The cursor, you remember, is the flashing box of light.

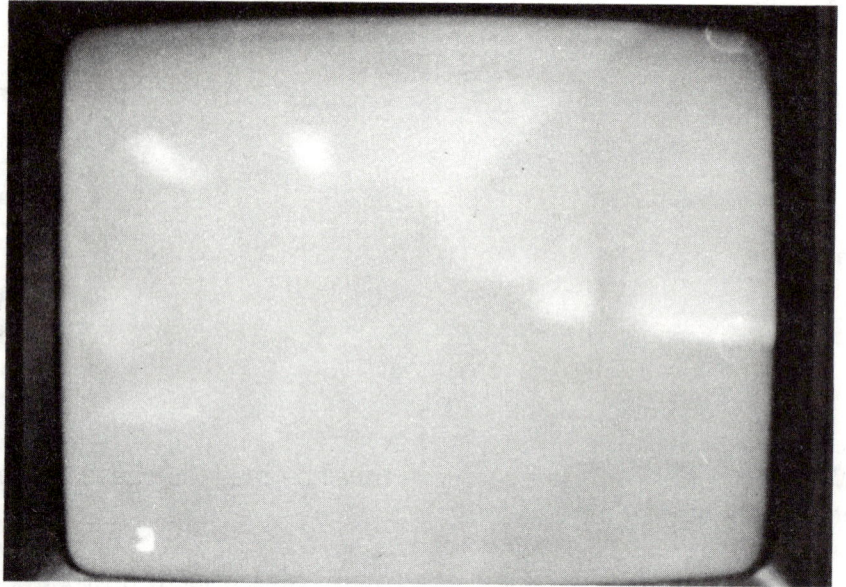

GR leaves the bottom four lines for words. We can see what we type along the bottom of the screen.

Now type the command COLOR=, but do not press the return key yet. We need to add a number after the = sign. In low-resolution graphics, we can choose from 16 colors.

Ø = black	8 = brown
1 = magenta	9 = orange
2 = dark blue	1Ø = gray
3 = purple	11 = pink
4 = dark green	12 = green
5 = gray	13 = yellow
6 = medium blue	14 = aqua
7 = light blue	15 = white

CHECK YOUR APPLESOFT TUTORIAL PAGE 18 FOR A COLOR CHART OF THE APPLE'S 16 COLORS.

Type 12 after the = sign and *R.

The screen looks the same, but now the computer is ready to draw in green.

In order to draw, we need commands. We will use just one command and save the other two for Chapter 3.

The command to turn on one light on the screen is PLOT. But we need two numbers for the PLOT command to work. The numbers tell the computer where to turn on the light.

If you look at your worksheet called EXPLORING PLOT WORKSHEET, you can see that the screen is made of many little boxes. We can turn on one, all, or just some of them.

Look at the worksheet closely. Across the top of the grid, you will see numbers. These numbers count the vertical (up and down) columns. These numbers are called the vertical counters.

There are also numbers which go down the left side of the grid. These numbers are called horizontal counters because they number the horizontal (across) rows.

The grid is numbered Ø to 39. That makes 40 boxes.

Each column and row has 40 boxes. They are really rectangles because they are longer than they are wide. But we will call them boxes just to keep things simple. Because it really is simple to draw with your Apple.

Now that you know how the screen is set up, let's use it.

As we go through this chapter, fill in the boxes we use with a pencil or colored pencil, if you want to be fancy.

Just as you have an address to show where you live, the little boxes also have numbers to show where they are located.

The address of each box contains two numbers.

The first number tells the computer how far to the right it will go.

The second number tells the computer how far down it will go.

REMEMBER: THE COMPUTER STARTS COUNTING WITH Ø. OUR FIRST COLUMN OR ROW WILL BE Ø, NOT 1.

PLOT RIGHT, DOWN

It is very important to have a comma between the numbers. If you forget the comma, the computer will not understand you. If you forget the comma, the computer will print SYNTAX ERROR on the screen. Retype the PLOT command and put the comma between the numbers and the computer will be happy and PLOT your light for you.

EXPLORING PLOT WORKSHEET

vertical
counters

horizontal
counters

0 1 2 3 4 5 6 7 8 9 10 11 12 13 14 15 16 17 18 19 20 21 22 23 24 25 26 27 28 29 30 31 32 33 34 35 36 37 38 39

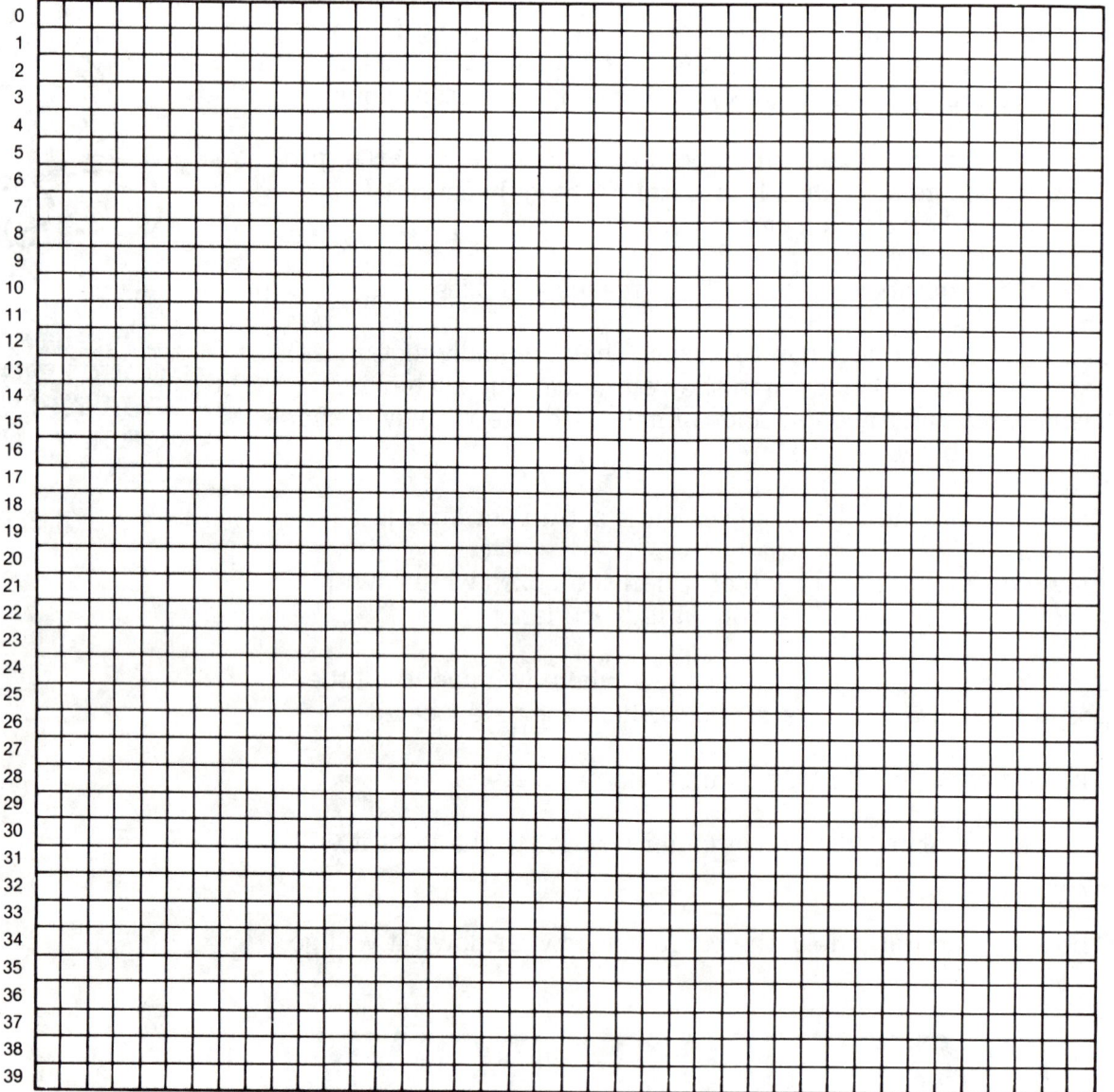

0
1
2
3
4
5
6
7
8
9
10
11
12
13
14
15
16
17
18
19
20
21
22
23
24
25
26
27
28
29
30
31
32
33
34
35
36
37
38
39

1. PLOT _____ , _____
2. PLOT _____ , _____
3. PLOT _____ , _____
4. PLOT _____ , _____

The computer knows where to turn on the lights because we tell it where to go. Let's do a PLOT and watch what happens.

Type PLOT Ø,Ø

REMEMBER:
PLOT ⟶____, ____↓
THE COMMA IS VERY
IMPORTANT.

What do you see? If you typed correctly, you should see a green box of light in the upper left corner of the screen.

The computer moved Ø to the right (the first number) and Ø down (the second number). Then it turned on the light.

Type PLOT 39,Ø

What do you see?

Another light has appeared. It should be in the upper right corner.

The computer moved 39 to the right and down Ø.

The bottom right corner would be?

Right!

PLOT 39,39

What command will put a green box of light in the bottom left corner?

The command would be: PLOT Ø,39.

SIMPLE?? YOU BET IT IS!!

Your worksheet should have the boxes in each corner filled in.

Let's experiment with another color.

Use any color you like.

To change colors, what do you type?

Right! COLOR= followed by the number of the color you want.

What's your favorite color?

Don't forget to press the return after you type the command to change your color.

Before you do more graphic exploring, we should talk about a four-step way to make your graphics easy to do.

To make our drawings the best they can be, we need to do four things.

1. **THINK** . . . . Think about your idea.
2. **PLAN** . . . . Plan it on the worksheet—fill in the boxes.
3. **WRITE** . . . . Write the commands. Use the COMMAND WORKSHEET to list your commands.
4. **DO** . . . . Do the typing of your commands on the keyboard.

By the way, there is a step five. It's called SMILE. You can do graphics.

Let's do this one together. Use the EXPLORING PLOT WORKSHEET.

I did the first two steps for you for this design.

1. **THINK** . . . . How about a flower?
2. **PLAN** . . . . I made a small four-plot flower.
3. **WRITE** . . . . . . : . Now we can write the commands.
   PLOT _____ , _____   REMEMBER:
   PLOT _____ , _____   How far over, how far down
   PLOT _____ , _____
   PLOT _____ , _____
4. **DO** . . . . Type the commands now.

Don't forget to press the return after each command.

EXPLORING PLOT WORKSHEET

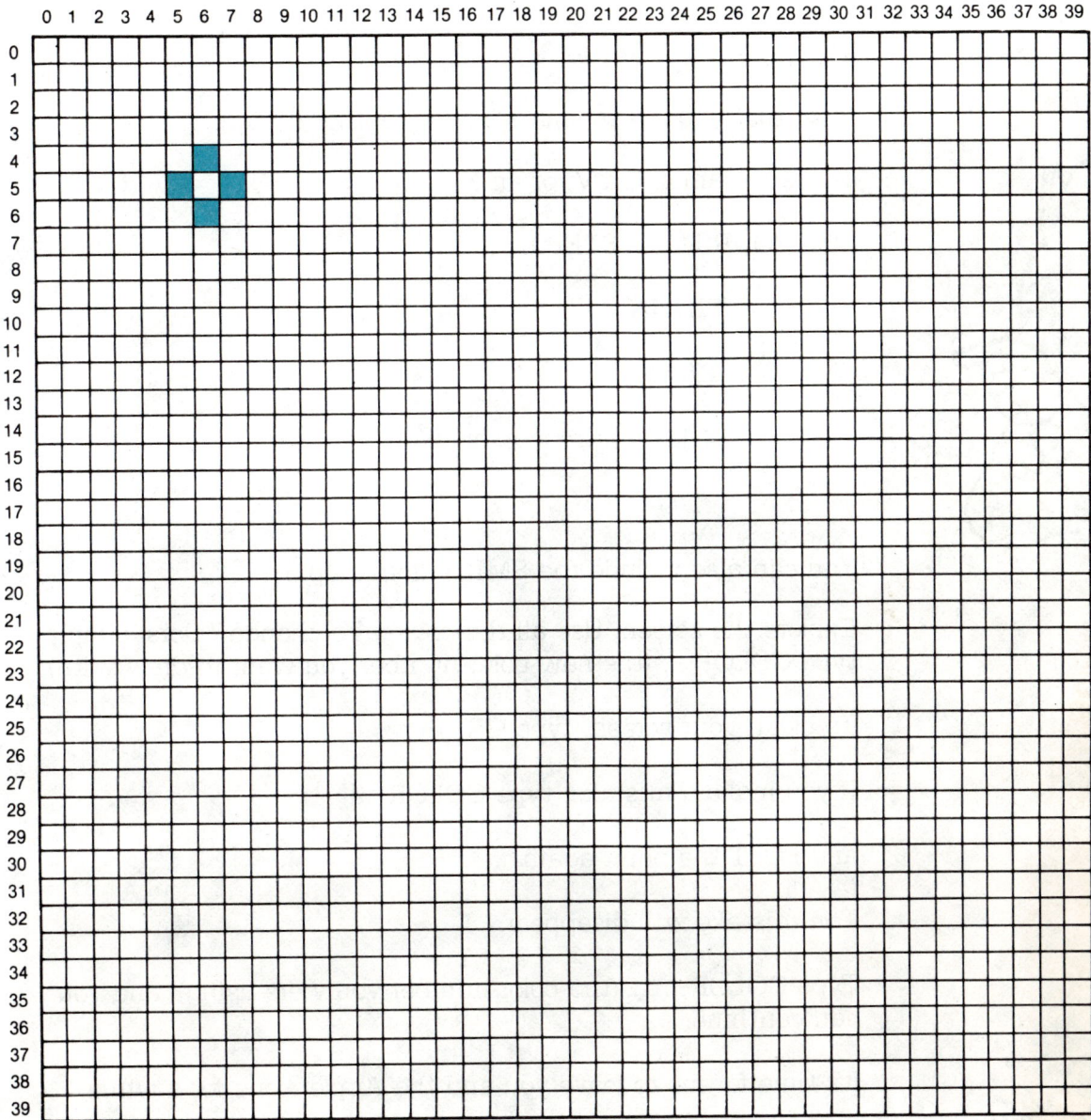

1. PLOT _____,_____
2. PLOT _____,_____
3. PLOT _____,_____
4. PLOT _____,_____

Your commands should be:

PLOT 6,4
PLOT 5,5
PLOT 6,6
PLOT 7,5

Now that you are so smart, make another design.

Make a diamond, a V, or an X.

USE YOUR FOUR STEPS:

THINK

PLAN

WRITE

DO

You can also include the SMILE from step 5.

Explore the screen. Use all the colors. To change colors, simply type COLOR=, (the new color number you want to draw with)

To clean your screen, type GR.

If you make a mistake, type COLOR=Ø

and PLOT the point again.

The mistake will disappear.

Type COLOR= __ (the color number you were using), and you can continue.

It's time for me to leave you and the Apple alone for a while.

In the next lesson, we will learn to draw lines. Lines will help us draw faster.

For now, enjoy PLOT!!

In review

Place the letter of the definition
in front of the word it describes.

_____ GR

_____ COLOR=

_____ PLOT _____ , _____

_____ VERTICAL COLUMNS

_____ HORIZONTAL ROWS

_____ THINK

_____ PLAN

_____ WRITE

_____ DO

_____ SMILE

a. what you do when you program in low-res graphics.
b. tells the computer to turn on one light on the screen.
c. tells the computer we want to draw on the screen.
d. rows that go across the grid on the worksheet and screen.
e. command followed by a number between Ø and 15 that tells the computer what color we want to draw with.
f. columns that go up and down on the grid on the worksheet and on the screen.
g. first thing we do when drawing in low-res graphics.
h. second thing we do when drawing in low-res graphics.
i. third thing we do when drawing in low-res graphics.
j. fourth thing we do when drawing in low-res graphics.

GRAPHIX GRADE BOX

CORRECT

8–10

5–7

0–4

Lines light the screen

3

Back for more already? I hope you enjoyed PLOT. I'm glad you're excited about programming in low-res. You will be even more excited after you learn how to draw lines on the screen. Make sure you have your computer on and we're on our way.

Later in this chapter, we will write and save our first color graphics program. It will be fast, fun and EASY!

At the end of chapter 2, we learned that PLOT makes the computer turn on one light at a time. Our next commands will make lines of light.

Our new commands will be VLIN (say Vee-line) and HLIN (say H-Line).

VLIN will draw vertical (up and down) lines.

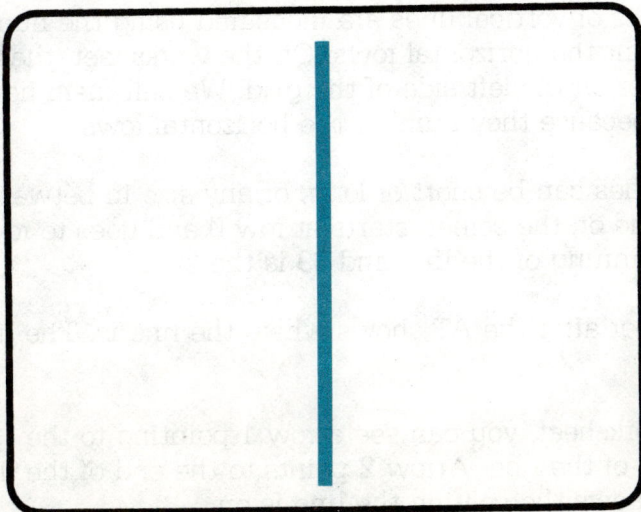

VEE-LINE AND H-LINE

HLIN will draw horizontal (across) lines.

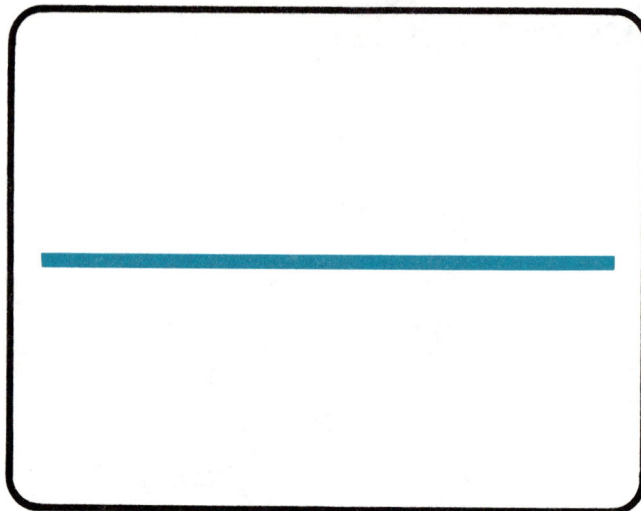

Let's type and talk as we go along.

Type: GR *R (remember to press the return)

COLOR= (the color you want)

We will draw a vertical line first.

Type this command: VLIN Ø,39 at Ø

What happened?

A vertical line appeared on the left side of the screen. How did the computer know to do that? It knew because you told it.

Look at the worksheet called EXAMPLE SHEET FOR VLIN.

The lengths of vertical lines are measured using the numbers which count the horizontal rows. On the worksheet, these are the number on the left side of the grid. We call them horizontal counters because they number the horizontal rows.

Vertical lines can be short or long, or any size in between. The vertical line on the screen starts at row Ø and goes to row 39. Ø is the beginning of the line and 39 is the end.

The number after the AT shows where the line is. The line is on column Ø.

On the worksheet, you can see arrow 1 pointing to the beginning of the line. Arrow 2 points to the end of the line. Arrow 3 shows the column the line is on.

EXAMPLE SHEET FOR VLIN

LENGTHS OF VERTICAL LINES ARE MEASURED BY
HORIZONTAL COUNTERS ON LEFT OF GRID.

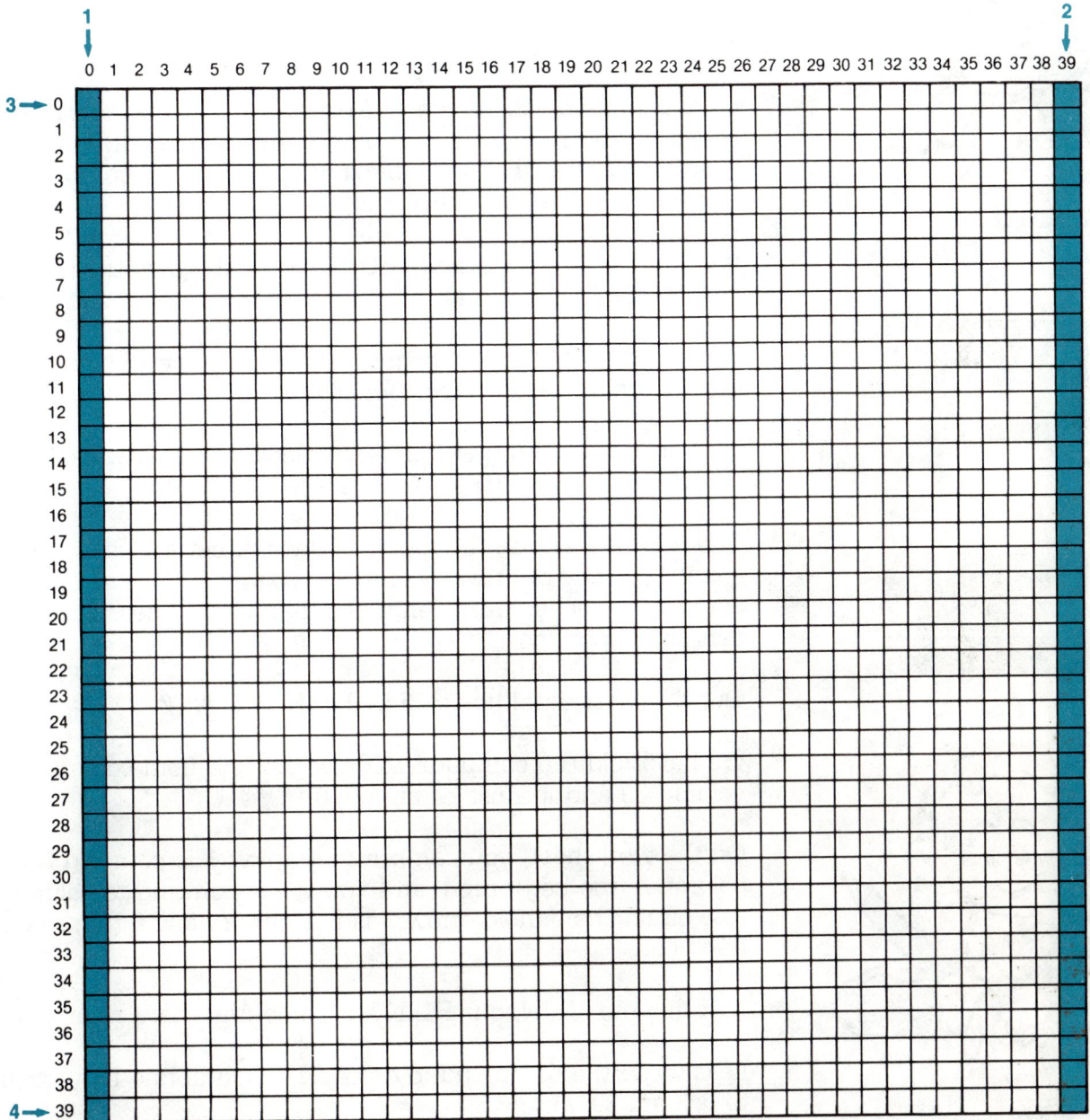

VLIN Ø,39 at Ø : starts at Ø (1)
               ends at 39 (2)
               on column Ø (3)

VLIN Ø,39 at 39 : starts at Ø
               ends at 39
               on column 39 (4)

Now we can understand what VLIN Ø,39 at Ø means to the
computer.

It draws a vertical line from row 0 to row 39 and makes sure that it is on column 0.

Let's put a vertical line on the other side of the screen. This line will also be from row 0 to row 39. But it must be at column *39*.

Type VLIN 0,39 at 39

Look at the worksheet again. Arrows 1 and 2 are the same because the line has the same beginning and end. It is the same length. But this time, the line is on column 39. The number that follows the AT is very important.

If you understand the beginning, end, and where the line is AT, you are ready to draw an HLIN.

We will need to know a beginning point, and end point, but this time, we also need to know what *row* the line is on.

Let's start by looking at our next worksheet. This worksheet is called EXAMPLE SHEET FOR HLIN.

The numbers across the top of the worksheet are called vertical counters. They number the vertical columns. We use the vertical counters to measure the lengths of horizontal lines. The lines can be long or short.

Our first horizontal line will be HLIN 0,39 AT 0

We have told the computer to draw the line from column 0 to column 39 and it must be on row 0.

On the worksheet, you can see that arrow 1 is pointing to column 0 (the beginning) and arrow 2 is pointing to column 39 (the end). The double arrow 3 is pointing to row 0 (the row the line is on).

Just like our VLIN, our HLIN has three important numbers.

Let's write the command to draw a horizontal line from column 0 to column 39 on row 39.

Did you say HLIN 0,39 AT 39?

You're correct as usual. I knew you would be able to do these VLINs and HLINs. You're brilliant!!!

Now it would be very boring to draw in just long V and HLINs, so let's practice making short and medium lines.

REMEMBER: THE COMPUTER STARTS COUNTING WITH 0, SO OUR FIRST COLUMN OR ROW WILL HAVE THE NUMBER 0.

REMEMBER: VLIN HAS THREE IMPORTANT PARTS, THE BEGINNING NUMBER, END NUMBER AND THE NUMBER THAT TELLS THE COMPUTER WHERE THE LINE IS AT.

EXAMPLE SHEET FOR HLIN

LENGTHS OF HORIZONTAL LINES ARE MEASURED BY THE
VERTICAL COUNTERS ACROSS THE TOP OF THE GRID.

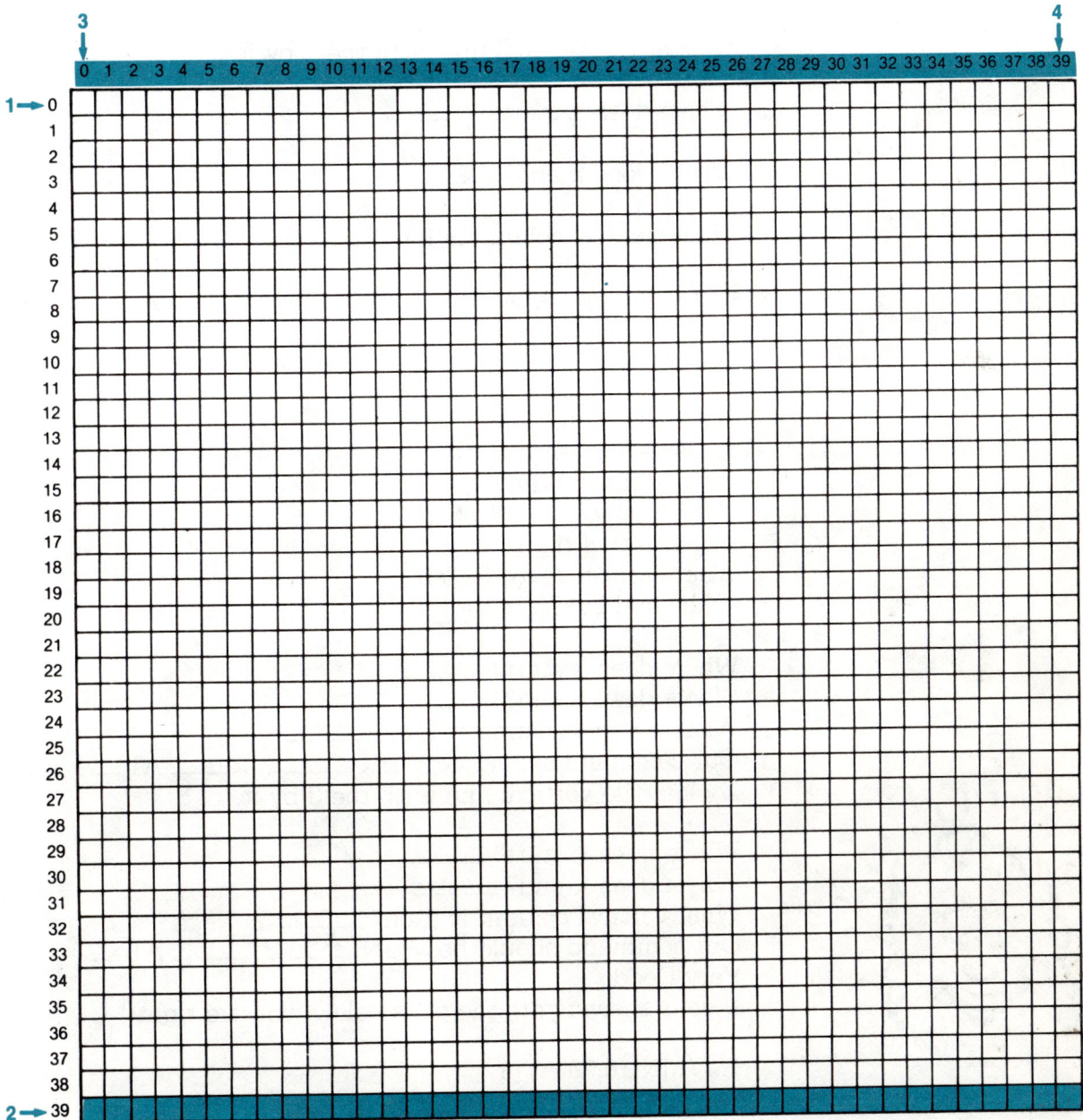

HLIN Ø,39 at Ø starts at Ø (1)
ends at 39 (2)
on row Ø (3)

HLIN Ø,39 at 39 starts at Ø
ends at 39
on row 39(4)

We can make lines any length we want.

Look at the worksheet called EXPERIMENTING WITH VLIN AND HLIN.

Can you write the commands for these vertical and horizontal lines? Type them into the computer as we work along.

Look at the vertical line with the 1 by it.

Where does it start? _____

Where does it end? _____

What vertical column is it on? _____

Our command should be VLIN _____,_____ AT __

Look at the vertical line with the 2 by it.

Horizontal counters
measure the lengths of
vertical lines. What
number is to the left of the
beginning of the line?
What number is to the left
of the end box?

Where does it start? _____
Where does it end? _____
What vertical column is it on? _____
Our command should be VLIN _____,_____ AT __
Look at the vertical line with the 3 by it.

Where does it start? _____
Where does it end? _____
What vertical column is it on? _____
Our command should be VLIN _____,_____ AT __
Very Good!
If your answers are the ones below, you are right!!

1. VLIN 10,20 AT 3
2. VLIN 1,5 AT 32
3. VLIN 22,23 AT 20

Now let's work on the horizontal lines.

Look at the horizontal line with the 1 by it.

Where does it start? _____

EXPERIMENTING WITH VLIN AND HLIN WORKSHEET

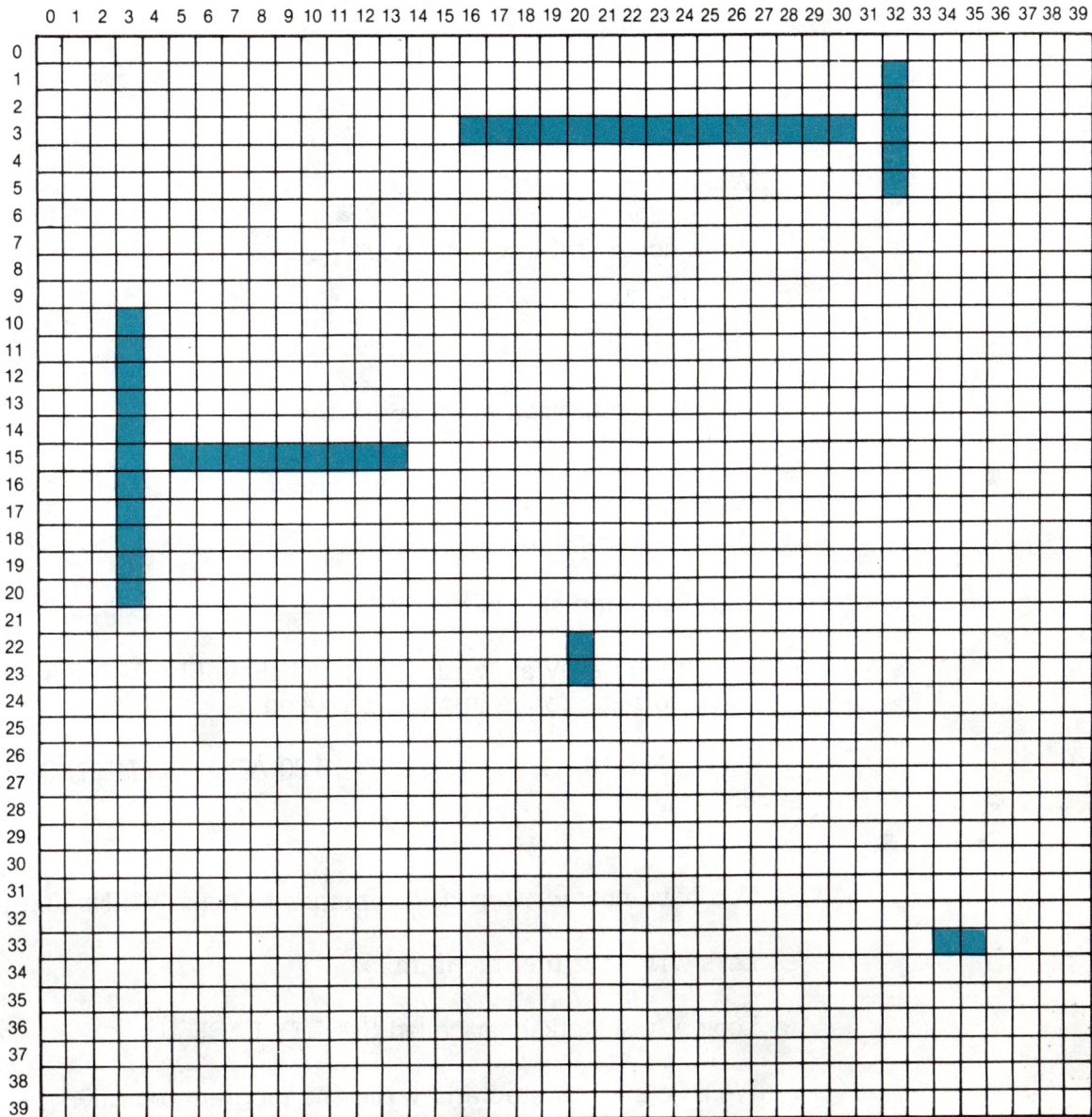

WHAT ARE THE COMMANDS FOR THE 3 VLINs AND 3
HLINs ON THIS WORKSHEET?

1. VLIN _____,_____ AT __
2. VLIN _____,_____ AT __
3. VLIN _____,_____ AT __

1. HLIN _____,_____ AT __
2. HLIN _____,_____ AT __
3. HLIN _____,_____ AT __

The vertical counters across the top
of the worksheet measure the length
of horizontal lines. What number is
above the beginning of the line?

Where does it end? What number is above the end box? _____

What horizontal row is it on? _____
Our command should be HLIN _____ , _____ AT __

Look at the horizontal line with the 2 by it.

Where does it start? _____
Where does it end? _____
What horizontal row is it on? _____

Our command should be HLIN _____ , _____ AT __

Look at the horizontal line with the 3 by it.

Where does it start? _____
Where does it end? _____
What horizontal row is it on? _____

Our command should be HLIN _____ , _____ AT __

Check your answers with the ones below. I bet you have them 100% correct. You're just too, too good.

1.) HLIN 5,13 AT 15   2.) HLIN 16,30 AT 3   3.) HLIN 34,35 AT 33

You have now written 10 commands to make VLINs and HLINs.

Let's write our first program.

Look at the worksheet called SMILEY FACE.

We'll go step by step and write the program together.

We'll also learn a few new commands as we go along.

Do you remember the plan to make our graphics better?

THINK. . . . . .I've thought of the picture for you.
PLAN. . . . . .I've planned most of it on the worksheet.
WRITE. . . . . . . .I've written some of the commands for you.
DO! . . . . .We're going to DO it now.

First, we need to clear off our experimental VLINs and HLINs.

SMILEY FACE

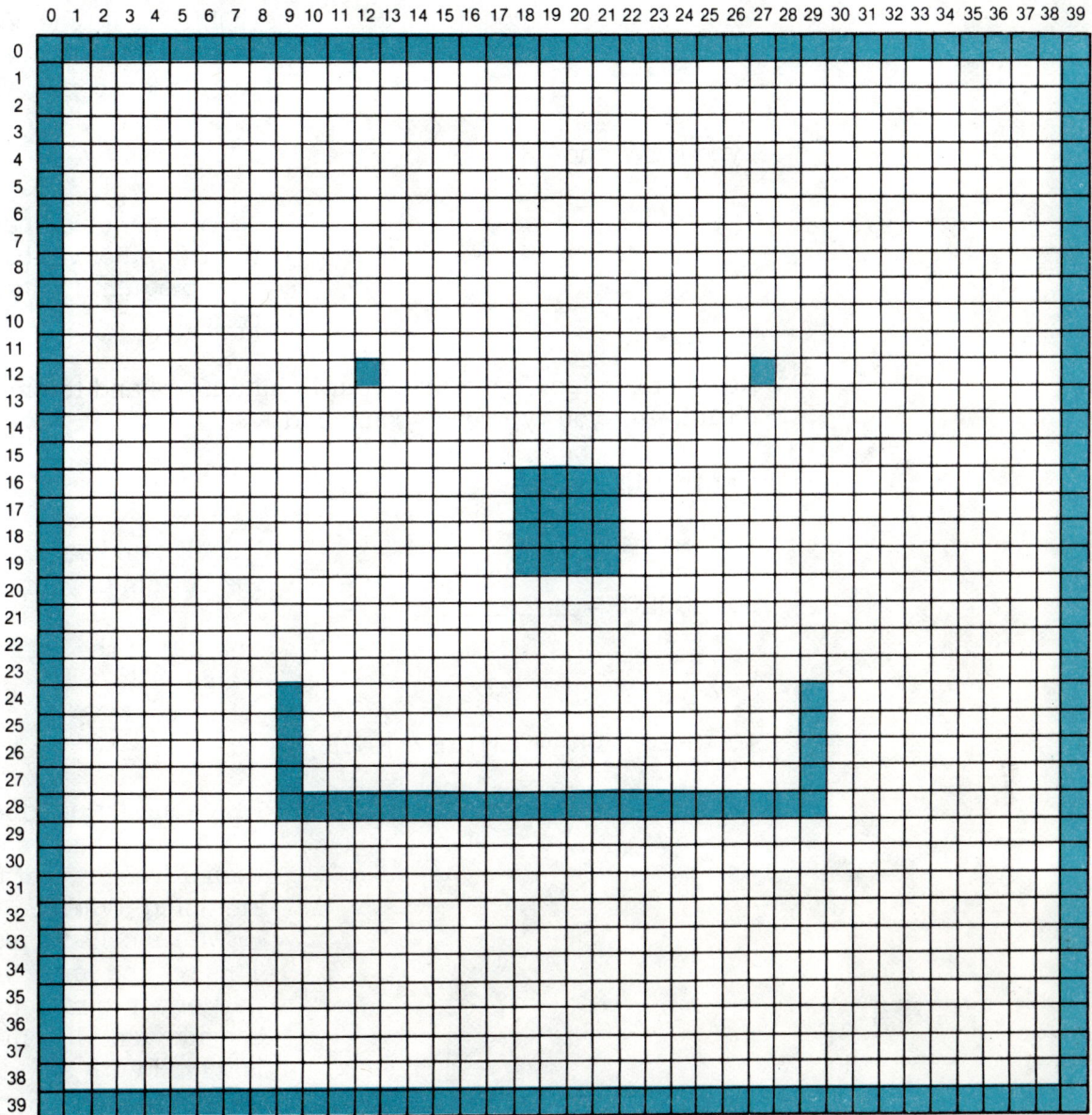

Type TEXT and *R (press the return)

TEXT takes the graphics off the screen. We are now on the text screen. Don't worry about the flashing.

Type HOME and *R

HOME clears the screen
and places the cursor at
the top left corner.

Type NEW and *R

NEW, you remember, tells
the computer we have a
new program for its
memory.

Now here we go. Remember your line numbers and to press the
return after you type each command.

Our first line will be

```
10   HOME
20   GR
30   COLOR= _____
```

HOME will keep words off
the bottom of your screen.

You put in the color you
want.

```
40   REM   DRAW SMILEY FACE
```

REMs are for us to read.
Good programmers remind
themselves of what they
are doing. When you type
REM, it's called a remark.
This will be important if
part of your program
doesn't work. If something
is wrong with a certain
part, you can read your
REMs and find the
commands that are wrong.

```
50   VLIN 0,39 AT 0
60   VLIN 0,39 AT 39
70   HLIN 0,39 AT 0
80   HLIN 0,39 AT 39
```

If you make an error in typing, it's OK. Just retype the line
number with the correct command. The computer will put it
in the correct order.

RUN tells the computer to do the program in its memory.

Now type RUN and *R

There is our rectangle again.
Type TEXT and *R
Now type the command LIST.

```
90 REM DRAW EYES
100 PLOT 12,12
110 PLOT ___,___
120 REM DRAW NOSE
```

Where are you going to put the other eye so they are even? How many commands will you need to draw the nose? I only gave you four lines. Will your lines be VLINs or HLINs?

**REMEMBER:
LIST TELLS THE
COMPUTER TO SHOW
US THE COMMANDS
OF OUR PROGRAM IN
NUMBER ORDER.**

```
130
140
150
160
170 REM DRAW MOUTH
```

How many commands will you need to draw the mouth? I only gave you three lines.

```
180
190
200
```

If you want more lines, do you remember how to do it? Use the numbers between the ones I've written down for you.
EXAMPLE: MORE MOUTH LINES
181,182,183,184,185, etc.

If you want a girl smiley face, you can add magenta cheeks and blue eye shadow.

Just add the REMs and the line numbers you need.

TEXT turns off graphics so you can see your commands.
LIST puts commands in order.

You can also type commands and see your program at the same time.

After you type RUN and *R

Type LIST

**REMEMBER: RUN lets you see how your drawing is growing.
TEXT turns off graphics so you can see your commands.
LIST puts commands in order.**

47

Your listing will be behind your picture. You will be able to see the last few lines of your program and see the one you are working on.

After you finish your commands, type RUN and LIST again.

It's fun to see your face grow.

If you want to see your listing to change the beginning of your program, you can tell the computer what commands to LIST.

If you type LIST 20,50 or LIST 20-50,
the computer will print just the commands from 20 to 50.

EXAMPLE: 20
             30
             40
             50

When you see the command you want to change, just retype it. If you want to add more commands as numbers in between, just type them.

It is easy to work with these command listings.

If you don't remember where a section is, you can use two other keys to help you.

The S key and the C key do nice things when you use them with the CTRL (CONTROL KEY) key.

The CTRL key changes what the S and C key do. There are other keys that work with the CTRL key we will learn about later.

After you type LIST, hold down the CTRL key and press the S key. The listing will STOP. Press the S key again and the listing will continue.

This will take practice. But that is why we are here.

The CTRL key with the C key will break the list. Type LIST, hold down the CTRL key, and press the C key. You can now add commands. Type LIST and the computer puts them in number order for you.

I'll leave you alone for a while. Finish up your smiley face and read on when you're done. We'll learn how to SAVE our smiley face.

The last command in your program should be:
_____ PRINT "SMILEY by _____ ."

SAVE tells the computer to record our program on the diskette in the drive.

IF THE NAMES ARE NOT DIFFERENT, THE FIRST PROGRAM WILL BE ERASED AS THE SECOND IS PLACED ON THE DISKETTE. THE FIRST PROGRAM WILL BE GONE. AND SOMEONE WOULD BE UPSET.

It is simple to save your program.

Type SAVE and the name of your program. Press the return. The disk drive will whir and your program will be recorded.

The name can be anything you like.

SAVE FACE

SAVE SM FACE

Try to keep your program name short and simple.

There you have it. Your program is safe. Let's check to be sure.

Type TEXT (to clear graphics.)

Type CATALOG and *R

CATALOG tells the computer to print out the names of the programs on the diskette.

REMEMBER: EVERY PROGRAM HAS A NAME. ITS NAME MUST BE DIFFERENT FROM ALL OTHER PROGRAM NAMES ON THE DISKETTE.

CATALOG tells the computer to print out the names of the programs on the diskette.

You should see two programs listed.

HELLO

and the one you saved.

Turn off your computer. Wait five seconds and turn it on again.

Type RUN (and the name of your program.)

You should see your smiley face.

Congratulations.

You have learned a lot. You're almost a pro programmer. After you look at Chapter 4, you will be ready to do the activities in Chapters 5 and 6.

Don't do all of them in one day. They will be even more fun after you do Chapters 7 and 8.

I need to rest. See you soon. And remember,

GRAPHICS ARE GREAT!!!

In review

Place the letter of the definition in front of the word it describes.

_____ VLIN _____, _____ AT _____

_____ HLIN _____, _____ AT _____

_____ HOME

_____ REM

_____ TEXT

_____ LIST

_____ SAVE

_____ LIST 2Ø,60

a. tells the computer to clear graphics from screen.
b. reminds us what our program does in certain line numbers.
c. clears a screen and places cursor at top left corner.
d. draws a vertical line.
e. makes a listing of program commands in number order.
f. draws a horizontal line.
g. tells the computer to save our program onto a diskette.
h. lists the program commands from line 2Ø to line 6Ø.

GRAPHIX GRADE BOX

CORRECT

7–8

4–6

0–3

Syntax errors
4

AIN'T I glad to see you!

You sure IS a sight for old eyes!

Holy mackerel! Who said that?

I haven't seen SYNTAX ERRORS like those in a long time.

Just as we learned to speak English and made mistakes, we can make mistakes in programming.

If we type a word the computer doesn't understand, it will print:

? SYNTAX ERROR

on the screen.

The question mark in front of the words SYNTAX ERROR is your clue that the computer doesn't understand what you typed.

Most ? SYNTAX ERRORS for beginners are typing errors. Let's look at a few of them.

```
GR
COLOR=12
POLT Ø,14
? SYNTAX ERROR
```

Misspelling PLOT gives us a . . . . . .

```
PLOT Ø 14
? SYNTAX ERROR
```

Leaving out a comma gives us a. . . . .

```
PLOT Ø,145
? ILLEGAL QUANTITY ERROR
```

A number larger than 39 gives us an . . . . . .

```
PLOT Ø,14
```

The computer plotted that one!!

There is another error you can run into. It is called the "MISSING COMMAND" error. That isn't what the computer says, but that's what I call it.

 It's the kind of SYNTAX ERROR that causes some confusion.

Type this short program, after you type NEW.

```
10 HOME
20 GR
30 COLOR=15
40 HLIN 5,34 AT 14
50 VLIN 5,34 AT 19
60 20,15
```

Leave out the PLOT command. It may happen to you.

```
70 20,39 AT 16
```

Leave out the HLIN command. It could happen to you.

Sometimes in the excitement of programming, we forget

the command because
we're in a hurry to see
what it will look like.
You know you don't have a
line number that large—so
what's the problem? The
mystery of the "MISSING
COMMAND!"

Type RUN

You will have a message printed to the screen. Can you guess
what it will be?

```
? SYNTAX ERROR IN 6020
```

You know you don't have
a line number that large—
so what's the problem? The
mystery of the "MISSING
COMMAND"!

Type TEXT

Type LIST

You should see the following listing:

```
10 HOME
20 GR
30 COLOR=15
40 HLIN 5,34 AT 14
50 VLIN 5,34 AT 19
6020  ,15
7020  ,39 AT 16
```

To rid your program of these strange numbers, type the
following.

Type 6020 and press the return key.
Type 7020 and press the return key.

Type RUN and the problem of the missing command is solved.

There is one other problem I would like you to know about. If
you know what this problem looks like, you can be on guard,
ready to fix it if it appears.

Add a new line 60.

`60 RUN`

Sometimes in the excitement of programming, we add RUN behind a line number. We might be too excited about seeing our program to see that a RUN has been typed instead of a command.

Type RUN

Notice how the computer runs the program over and over. It appears to be flashing. Actually it is being RUN time and time again.

Stop the program with a CTRL-C. Hold down the CTRL key and press the C key.

There. It's stopped.

You can also remove this problem by typing 60 and pressing the return key.

I can't possibly show you all the errors programmers can make. I just wanted you to see some of the popular ones some of my friends made.

You will make some errors, but you are prepared to fix them.

Other errors you will make and learn to fix yourself.

Just remember the ABCs of programming and you'll do fine.

What are the ABCs of programming??

```
A   B   C

  L E A
                    Always
  W     R

  A     E           Be

    Y     F
                    Careful
      S     U

          L
```

ON TO CHAPTER 5 AND THE REAL FUN!!!!!!!!!!!!

Supplement to Chapter 4

Before you start your A–Z lessons, let's do a short lesson together. For this activity you will use the worksheets labeled INITIALS IN A SQUARE and the WRITE COMMAND WORKSHEET with INITIALS IN A SQUARE-FIRST PROGRAM on it.

For your first program, let's put your initials in a square. The WRITE COMMAND WORKSHEET has the commands you need to draw the square.

Fill in the boxes inside the square with your initials. If you have a short name, try fitting your name in the square. Remember to use the entire box when drawing a design. You can't use half a box. You must use the whole box, as I did to make the square.

After your initials are finished, write the commands that will create them. Have your teacher correct your commands before you type them in.

Type NEW and you are ready to program your INITIALS IN A SQUARE. SAVE your program on a diskette. You may want to improve it later. SAVE it under your name. I SAVEd mine as M. Graphix. M stands for Mr.

INITIALS IN A SQUARE: FIRST PROGRAM

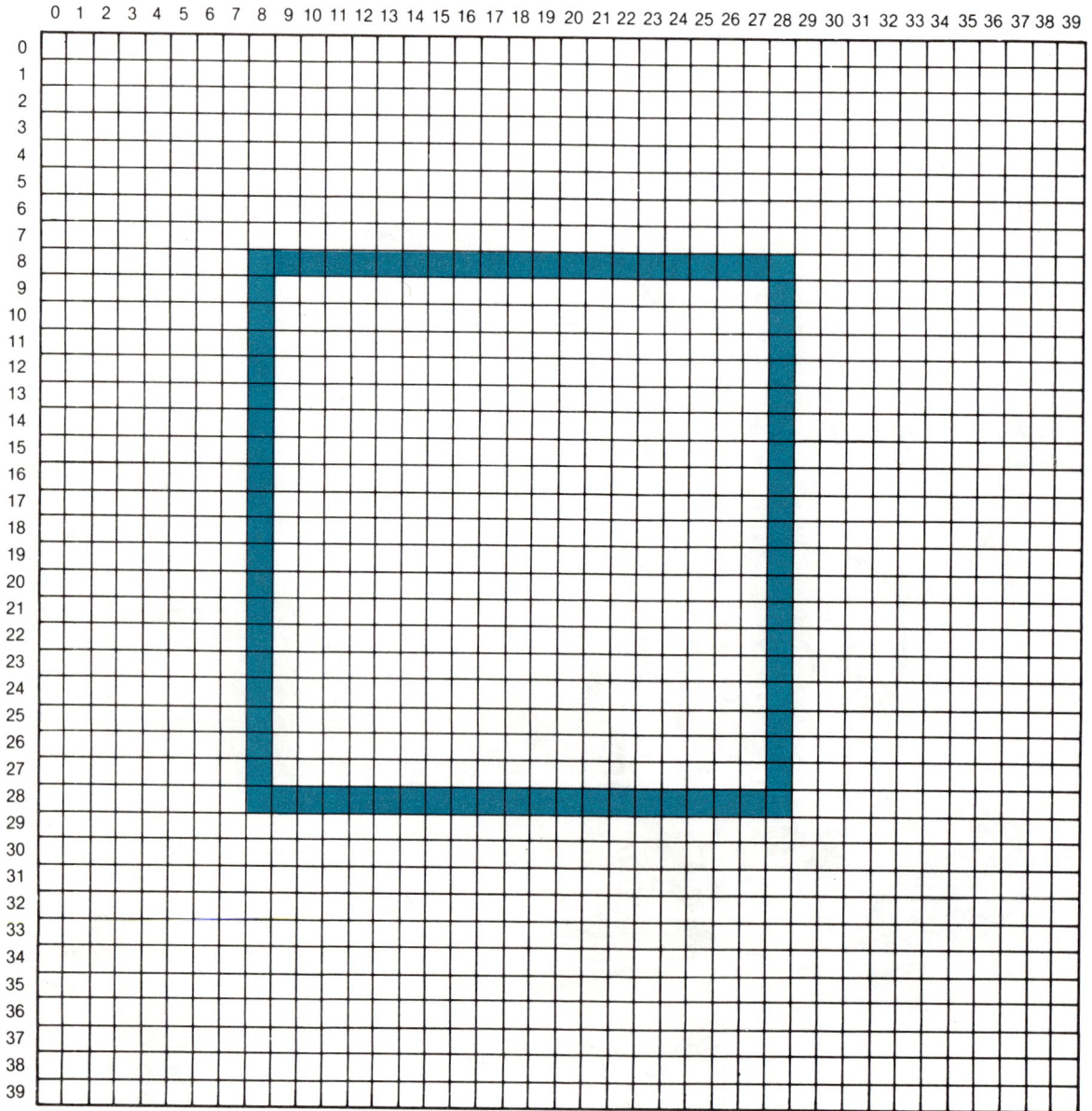

WRITE COMMANDS WORKSHEET

10	GR	260		510	
20	COLOR= your choice	270		520	
30	VLIN 8,28 at 8	280		530	
40	VLIN 8,28 at 28	290		540	
50	HLIN 8,28 at 8	300		550	
60	HLIN 8,28 at 28	310		560	
70		320		570	
80		330		580	
90		340		590	
100		350		600	
110		360		610	
120		370		620	
130		380		630	
140		390		640	
150		400		650	
160		410		660	
170		420		670	
180		430		680	
190		440		690	
200		450		700	
210		460		710	
220		470		720	
230		480		730	
240		490		740	
250		500		750	

Now that you have the commands for graphics under your belt, you can practice with them. The two games that follow are based on PLOT and VLIN and HLIN.

The first game is called GRID PLOT. It will help you practice with PLOT on the screen.

The second game has two versions. The first is called LINE PLOTTER. It draws vertical and horizontal lines on the screen. The second version is called LINE PLOTTER2. It draws lines too. But this version asks for the beginning and ending points of the line.

To play the games, you must type them into the computer. You won't understand some of the commands yet, but you will understand the games.

I hope you have fun with them. They're just for you.

Type NEW and press the return.

Type the following commands exactly as you see them.

Here's GRID PLOT:

```
10    REM   DRAW THE BACKGROUND
20    GR
30    COLOR= 15
40    FOR X = 0 TO 39
50    HLIN 0,39 AT X
60    NEXT X
70    REM   DRAW THE GRID
80    COLOR= 12
90    VLIN 0,39 AT 0
100   VLIN 0,39 AT 13
110   VLIN 0,39 AT 27
120   VLIN 0,39 AT 39
130   HLIN 0,39 AT 0
140   HLIN 0,39 AT 13
150   HLIN 0,39 AT 27
160   HLIN 0,39 AT 39
170   REM   SET WORKING COLOR TO BLACK
180   COLOR= 0
190   REM   GET READY FOR DIRECTIONS
200   HOME
210   PRINT "TRY TO PLACE A BLACK DOT IN"
220   PRINT "EACH WHITE SQUARE."
230   FOR P = 1 TO 2000: NEXT P
240   REM   PLOT THE BLACK SQUARES
250   INPUT "HOW FAR RIGHT? ";R
```

```
260    INPUT "HOW FAR DOWN? ";D
270    PLOT R,D
280    REM   DO IT AGAIN
290    HOME
300    GOTO 250
```

When you have finished, type RUN. When you are sure the game works, type:

SAVE GRID PLOT

RULES

Don't let any dots land on the green grid lines. Place one dot in each square.

You can use the GRID PLOT WORKSHEET as a guide to place the dots.

After you are a champion at *this* grid plot, have one of your friends change the VLINs and HLINs AT 13 and 27 in this program.

Figure 4–10 will help you.

The two VLIN commands to CHANGE are on lines 100 and 110. The two HLIN commands to CHANGE are on lines 140 and 150.

EXAMPLE:

Type CTRL C and press return key to break into the program. (You may also use your reset key.)

Type TEXT

Type LIST 100–150

Type

```
100    VLIN 0,39 AT 8
110    VLIN 0,39 AT 22
140    HLIN 0,39 AT 6
150    HLIN 0,39 AT 26
```

You can add even more VLINs and HLINs. You can have six or eight of each. Put them where you want them. Make the game difficult. See how many tries it takes you to put one black dot in each white space.

GRID PLOT WORKSHEET

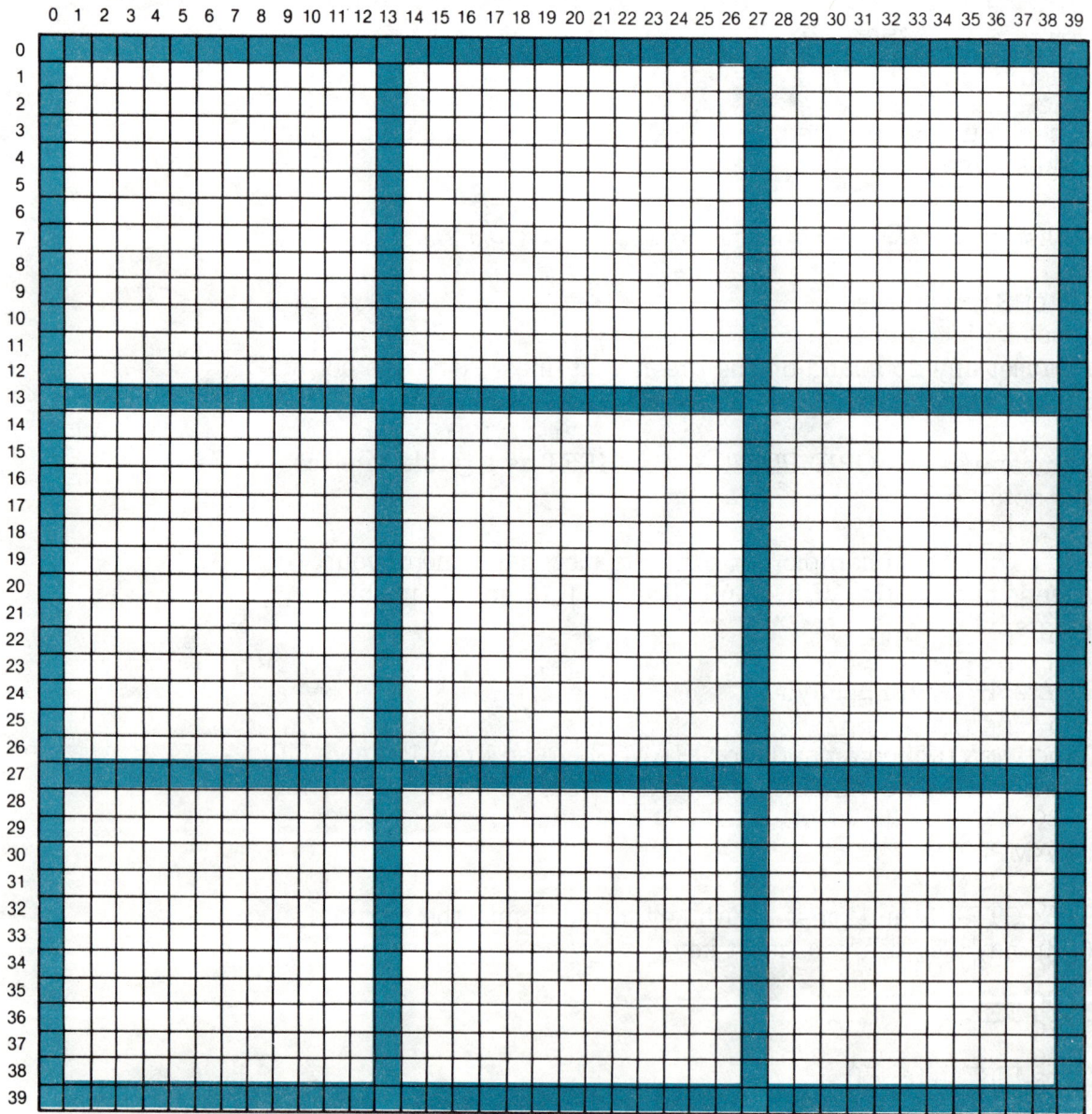

ALTERATIONS

Have a friend change the command lines which draw VLINs and HLINs AT 13 and 27. Make the changes so the program is different each time.

Type CTRL C to break into the program. Type LIST to see the commands that make GRID PLOT.

If you like your NEW version better than this one, type SAVE GRID PLOT and it will be on your disk.

Don't look when one of your friends types in the new VLINs and HLINs. It will be a real challenge for you to put one black dot in each of the new white areas. If you don't know how far apart the lines are, the game will be trickier than this one.

Have fun with GRID PLOT.

When you are ready for game two, come back for instructions.

I hope you enjoyed GRID PLOT. LINE PLOTTER is different. It uses VLINs and HLINs. Here are the commands to make the game. Again, type them in as they are. Don't forget to type NEW before you start.

```
10    HOME
20    PRINT " HI KIDS!"
30    PRINT : PRINT
40    PRINT "HERE IS A GAME FOR YOU!"
50    PRINT : PRINT : PRINT
60    PRINT "LET'S DRAW LINES."
70    PRINT : PRINT
80    PRINT "ARE YOU READY?"
90    PRINT : PRINT : PRINT
100   PRINT "PRESS SPACE BAR TO START."
110   GET A$
120   IF A$ =  CHR$ (32) THEN 140
130   GOTO 110
140   GR
150   PRINT : PRINT : PRINT
160   REM  CHOOSE COLOR
170   INPUT "WHAT COLOR DO YOU WANT?";C
180   COLOR= C
190   IF C > 15 THEN  GOTO 470
200   REM  PICK VER OR HOR LINES
210   HOME
220   PRINT "PRESS H FOR HORIZONTAL LINES."
230   PRINT "PRESS V FOR VERTICAL LINES."
240   GET A$
250   IF A$ =  CHR$ (72) THEN 390
260   IF A$ =  CHR$ (86) THEN 310
270   GOTO 240
280   PRINT : PRINT : PRINT
290   COLOR= C
300   REM  TO BUILD A VLIN
310   HOME
320   INPUT "HOW LONG OF A LINE?";L
330   INPUT "HOW FAR TO THE RIGHT?";R
340   HOME
```

```
350    PRINT "VLIN 0, ";L;" AT ";R;: VLIN 0,L AT
       R
360    FOR P = 1 TO 2000: NEXT P
370    GOTO 150
380    REM   TO BUILD A HLIN
390    HOME
400    INPUT "HOW LONG? ";L
410    INPUT "HOW FAR DOWN?";D
420    HOME
430    PRINT "HLIN 0,";L;" AT ";D: HLIN 0,L AT D
440    FOR P = 1 TO 2000: NEXT P
450    HOME
460    GOTO 150
470    PRINT : PRINT
480    PRINT " PLEASE USE A NUMBER BETWEEN 1 AND
       15!"
490    GOTO 150
```

As I promised you, there is a second version of LINE PLOTTER.
It is called LINE PLOTTER2.

This time you can tell the computer which number the line
begins and ends on. You will also tell it where to place the line.

Here are the commands. Type them in carefully. Each game will
help you become more familiar with the screen. As your skills
grow, the units A–Z will become even easier.

```
10     HOME
20     PRINT " HI KIDS!"
30     PRINT : PRINT
40     PRINT "HERE IS A GAME FOR YOU."
50     PRINT : PRINT : PRINT
60     PRINT "LET'S DRAW LINES."
70     PRINT : PRINT
80     PRINT "ARE YOU READY?"
90     PRINT : PRINT : PRINT
100    PRINT "PRESS SPACE BAR TO START."
110    GET A$
120    IF A$ =   CHR$ (32) THEN 140
130    GOTO 110
140    GR
150    PRINT : PRINT : PRINT
160    REM   CHOOSE COLOR
170    INPUT "WHAT COLOR DO YOU WANT?";C
180    COLOR= C
190    IF C > 15 THEN   GOTO 490
200    REM   PICK VER OR HOR LINES
210    HOME
220    PRINT "PRESS H FOR HORIZONTAL LINES."
230    PRINT "PRESS V FOR VERTICAL LINES."
240    GET A$
```

```
250   IF A$ =   CHR$ (72) THEN 400
260   IF A$ =   CHR$ (86) THEN 310
270   GOTO 240
280   PRINT : PRINT : PRINT
290   COLOR= C
300   REM  TO BUILD A VLIN
310   HOME
320   INPUT "WHERE WILL IT BEGIN? ";B
330   INPUT "WHERE WILL IT  END? ";E
340   INPUT "AT WHICH VERTICAL COUNTER?";VC
350   HOME
360   PRINT "VLIN ";B;" , ";E;" AT ";VC: VLIN B,
      E AT VC
370   FOR P = 1 TO 2000: NEXT P
380   GOTO 150
390   REM  TO BUILD A HLIN
400   HOME
410   INPUT "WHERE WILL IT BEGIN? ";B
420   INPUT "WHERE WILL IT END? ";E
430   INPUT "AT WHICH HORIZONTAL COUNTER? ";HC
440   HOME
450   PRINT "HLIN ";B;" , ";E;" AT ";HC: HLIN B,
      E AT HC
460   FOR P = 1 TO 2000: NEXT P
470   HOME
480   GOTO 150
490   PRINT : PRINT
500   PRINT " PLEASE USE A NUMBER BETWEEN 1  AND
      15!"
510   GOTO 150
```

Have fun with all three games. You may SAVE all of them on the same disk. You can call it your GAME practice disk. You didn't know practice could be so much fun, did you?

Activity units
A—M
5

APPLE
BOAT
CUBE
DOG
EGG YOLK
FISH
GHOST
HOUSE
INK
JACK-O-LANTERN
KEYS
LAMP
MONSTER

Before you start creating all your wonderful graphics, I want to tell you two things.

1. Use the plan to make your graphics better.
    A. THINK about your design
    B. PLAN your design on the worksheets with pencil or colored pencils
    C. WRITE your commands on the WRITE COMMANDS WORKSHEET
    D. DO your typing to create your program

Write your commands at home, not in front of the computer. Later after you have more experience, you will be able to compose pictures at the keyboard.

2. ENJOY! ENJOY! ENJOY!

NOTE TO TEACHER OR PARENT

Encourage children to write commands before they sit in front of the computer to program. My most able friends got into this habit and they made many programs they were proud of. They didn't waste time thinking in front of the computer. They were busy programming instead.

Encourage children to use the 4 steps I have explained.

THINK   PLAN   WRITE   DO

Give some class time for thinking, planning, and writing.

Class time can be a valuable aid for making computer time mostly DOing.

Students can check each other's work, too. It's helpful and a good learning experience for them.

apple

```
10    HOME
20    GR
30    REM   DRAW LARGE A
40    COLOR= 12
50    VLIN 1,5 AT 1
60    HLIN 2,3 AT 1
70    VLIN 2,5 AT 3
80    PLOT 2,3
90    REM   DRAW SMALL A
100   VLIN 2,5 AT 6
110   HLIN 7,8 AT 2
120   VLIN 3,5 AT 8
130   PLOT 7,4
140   REM   DRAW LEAF
150   PLOT 22,5
160   HLIN 20,21 AT 6
170   HLIN 19,21 AT 7
180   HLIN 18,20 AT 8
190   REM   DRAW STEM
200   COLOR= 8
210   VLIN 8,10 AT 17
220   VLIN 8,10 AT 16
230   VLIN 6,9 AT 15
240   REM   DRAW APPLE
250   COLOR= 1
260   HLIN 11,14 AT 10
270   HLIN 15,20 AT 11
280   HLIN 21,25 AT 12
290   HLIN 26,28 AT 13
300   VLIN 14,23 AT 29
310   PLOT 28,24
320   VLIN 25,26 AT 27
330   VLIN 27,28 AT 26
340   PLOT 25,29: PLOT 24,30
350   HLIN 12,23 AT 31
360   PLOT 12,30: PLOT 11,29
370   VLIN 27,28 AT 10
380   VLIN 25,26 AT 9
390   PLOT 8,24
400   VLIN 14,23 AT 7
410   PLOT 8,13: PLOT 9,12: PLOT 1
      0,11
420   END
```

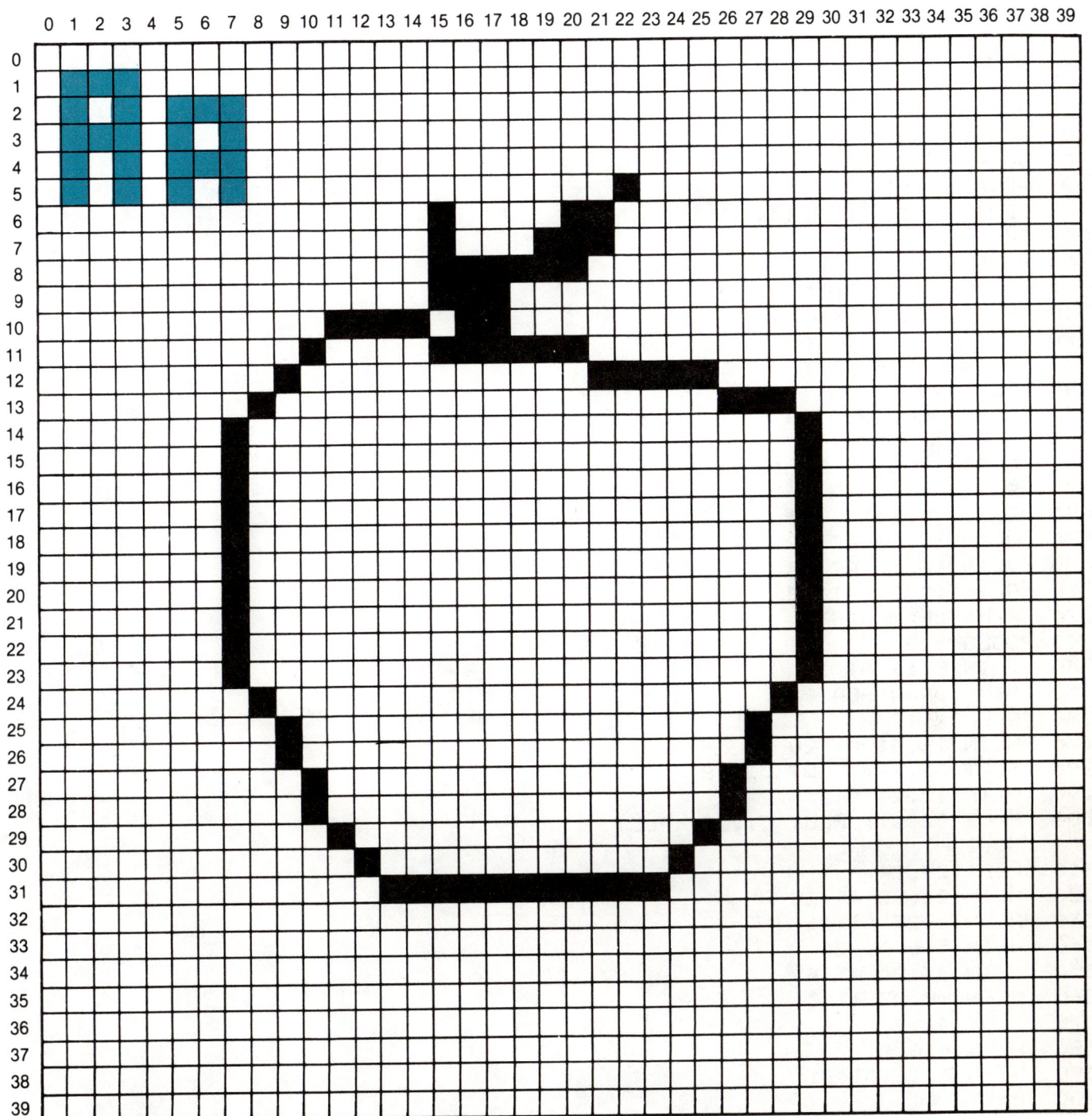

ALTERATIONS:
Fill in apple completely
Make a green apple
Does your apple have a worm in it?

Add   A words inside apple:
      ace, ant, ax.
Can you fit more words inside?

boat

```
10    HOME
20    GR
30    COLOR= 2
40    REM   DRAW BIG B
50    VLIN 1,6 AT 11
60    HLIN 12,13 AT 1
70    PLOT 12,3: PLOT 13,2
80    PLOT 12,6
90    VLIN 4,6 AT 13
100   REM   DRAW SMALL B
110   VLIN 2,6 AT 16
120   HLIN 17,18 AT 4
130   HLIN 17,18 AT 6
140   PLOT 18,5
150   REM   DRAW BOAT'S SAIL
160   COLOR= 15
170   PLOT 17,8: PLOT 18,9: PLOT 1
      9,10
180   VLIN 12,13 AT 21
190   VLIN 14,15 AT 22
200   VLIN 16,18 AT 23
210   HLIN 17,22 AT 18
220   REM   DRAW MAST
230   COLOR= 8
240   VLIN 8,19 AT 16
250   REM   DRAW BOAT
260   COLOR= 12
270   HLIN 16,31 AT 20
280   PLOT 31,19: PLOT 32,18
290   VLIN 17,20 AT 33
300   PLOT 32,21: PLOT 31,22: PLOT
      30,23
310   PLOT 29,24
320   HLIN 26,28 AT 25
330   HLIN 6,25 AT 26
340   HLIN 5,6 AT 25
350   VLIN 23,24 AT 4
360   VLIN 18,22 AT 3
370   PLOT 4,19
380   HLIN 4,6 AT 20
390   HLIN 6,16 AT 21
400   END
```

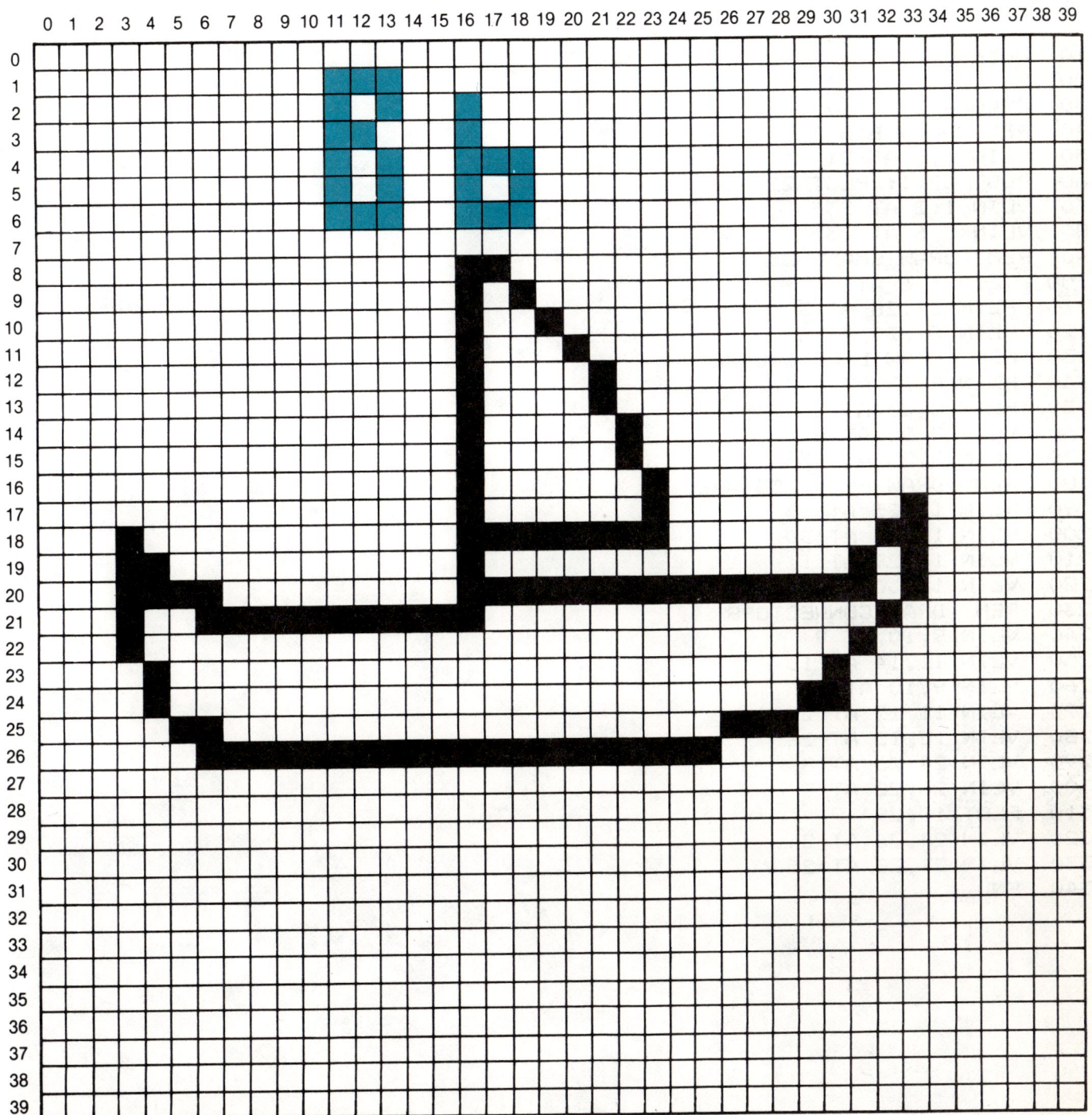

ALTERATIONS:
Add a sun or the moon.
Make the mast green.
Make the boat brown.
Put a rock in front of the boat.

Write boat across the bottom of the boat.

cube

```
10    HOME
20    GR
30    COLOR= 5
40    REM   DRAW BIG C
50    VLIN 1,6 AT 21
60    PLOT 22,1: PLOT 22,6
70    VLIN 1,2 AT 23
80    VLIN 5,6 AT 23
90    REM   DRAW SMALL C
100   VLIN 3,6 AT 26
110   HLIN 27,28 AT 3
120   HLIN 27,28 AT 6
130   REM   DRAW BACK SQUARE
140   HLIN 8,23 AT 8
150   HLIN 8,23 AT 23
160   VLIN 8,23 AT 8
170   VLIN 8,23 AT 23
180   REM   DRAW FRONT SQUARE
190   HLIN 11,25 AT 15
200   HLIN 11,25 AT 30
210   VLIN 16,29 AT 11
220   VLIN 16,30 AT 26
230   REM   DRAW CONNECTORS
240   VLIN 9,10 AT 9
250   VLIN 11,14 AT 10
260   VLIN 9,10 AT 24
270   VLIN 11,12 AT 25
280   VLIN 13,15 AT 26
290   VLIN 24,25 AT 8
300   VLIN 26,28 AT 9
310   PLOT 10,29
320   VLIN 24,26 AT 24
330   VLIN 27,28 AT 25
340   END
```

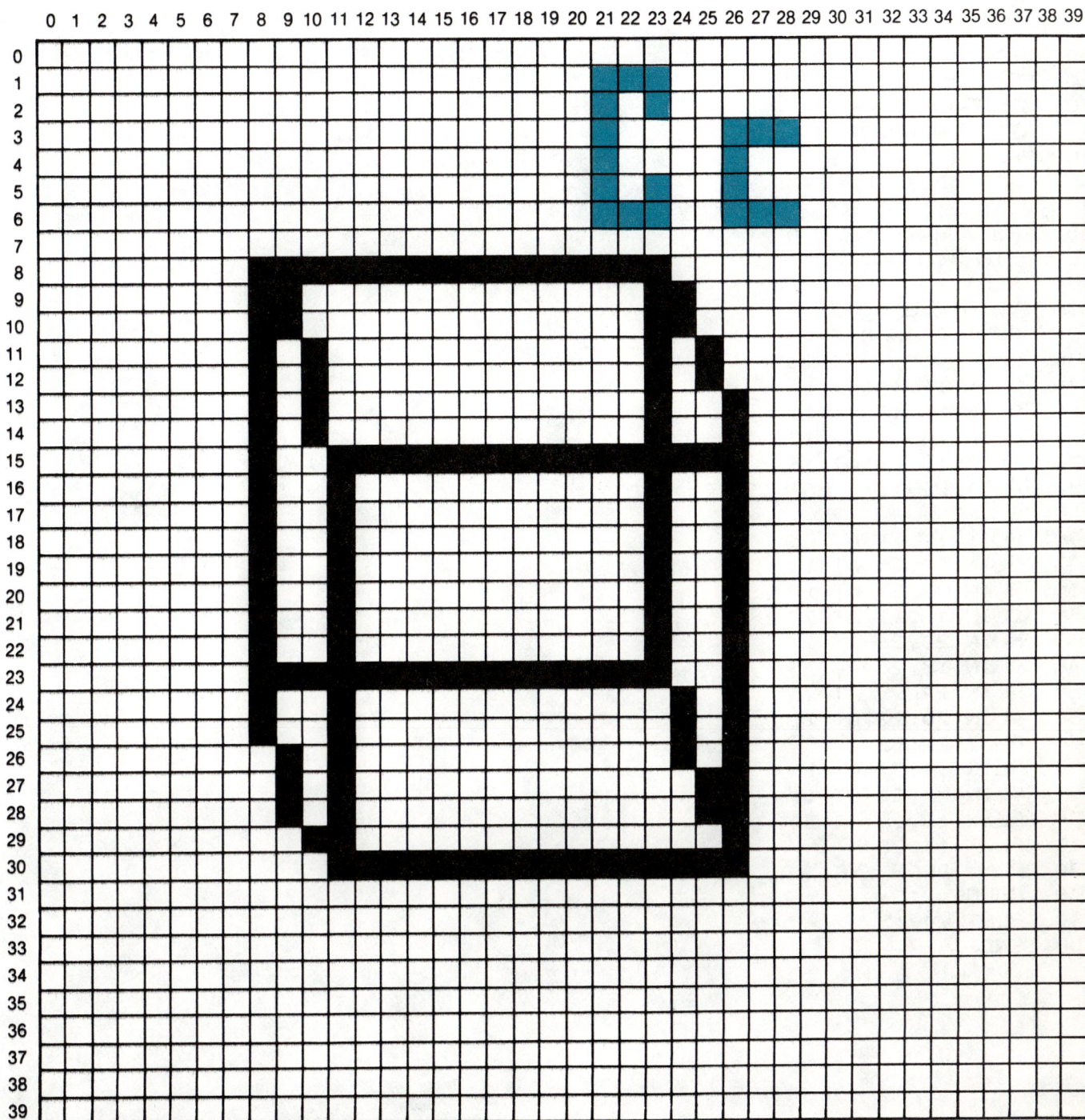

ALTERATIONS:

Make the front of the cube green.
Make the top of the cube light blue.
Make the left side of the cube dark blue.

Make the cube an alphabet block. Put your initials on it, one on top, one on the front.

dog

```
10   HOME
20   GR
30   COLOR= 13
40   REM   DRAW BIG D
50   VLIN 1,6 AT 31
60   PLOT 32,1: PLOT 32,6
70   VLIN 2,5 AT 33
80   REM   DRAW SMALL D
90   VLIN 4,6 AT 36
100   PLOT 37,4: PLOT 37,6
110   VLIN 2,6 AT 38
120   REM   DRAW DOG
130   COLOR= 8
140   VLIN 11,14 AT 11
150   VLIN 15,19 AT 12
160   VLIN 16,23 AT 13
170   HLIN 14,21 AT 16
180   PLOT 22,15: PLOT 22,13: PLOT
      21,12
190   VLIN 12,14 AT 23
200   HLIN 24,25 AT 14
210   HLIN 26,27 AT 15
220   VLIN 16,17 AT 27
230   HLIN 23,26 AT 17
240   VLIN 18,23 AT 23
250   HLIN 24,25 AT 23
260   VLIN 20,22 AT 21
270   PLOT 22,22
280   HLIN 14,22 AT 19
290   VLIN 17,24 AT 11
300   HLIN 12,13 AT 24
310   PLOT 14,23
320   REM   DRAW EYE
330   COLOR= 15
340   PLOT 24,15
350   END
```

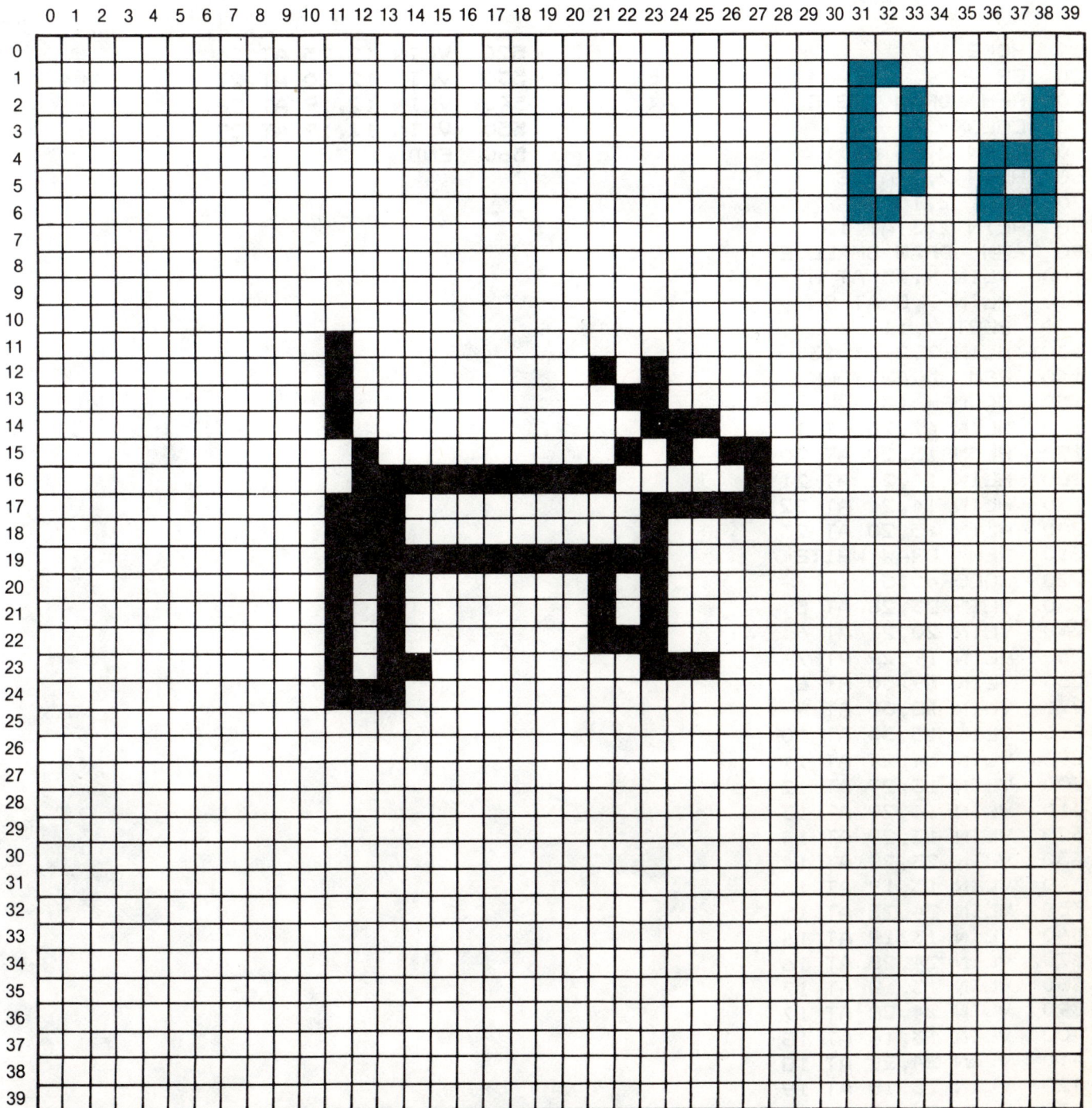

ALTERATIONS:
Add a tree.
Add a bone.
Add a doggie bowl.
What's the name of the dog?
Print his name, or hers, in graphics.

egg yolk

```
10    HOME
20    GR
30    REM   DRAW BIG E
40    COLOR= 3
50    VLIN 8,13 AT 1
60    HLIN 2,3 AT 8
70    PLOT 2,10
80    HLIN 2,3 AT 13
90    REM   DRAW SMALL E
100   VLIN 9,13 AT 6
110   HLIN 7,8 AT 9
120   PLOT 7,11
130   HLIN 7,8 AT 13
140   REM   DRAW YOLK
150   COLOR= 13
160   HLIN 17,20 AT 19
170   HLIN 15,20 AT 20
180   HLIN 14,21 AT 21
190   HLIN 14,21 AT 22
200   HLIN 15,20 AT 23
210   REM   DRAW WHITE
220   COLOR= 15
230   VLIN 23,26 AT 5
240   VLIN 20,27 AT 6
250   VLIN 19,29 AT 7
260   VLIN 19,30 AT 8
270   VLIN 18,30 AT 9
280   VLIN 15,30 AT 10
290   VLIN 14,29 AT 11
300   VLIN 13,29 AT 12
310   VLIN 14,29 AT 13
320   VLIN 13,20 AT 14
330   VLIN 23,29 AT 14
340   VLIN 13,19 AT 15
350   VLIN 24,28 AT 15
360   VLIN 13,19 AT 16
370   VLIN 24,28 AT 16
380   VLIN 13,18 AT 17
390   VLIN 24,28 AT 17
400   VLIN 13,18 AT 18
410   VLIN 24,28 AT 18
420   VLIN 13,18 AT 19
430   VLIN 24,28 AT 19
440   VLIN 13,18 AT 20
450   VLIN 24,28 AT 20
460   VLIN 12,20 AT 21
470   VLIN 23,27 AT 21
480   VLIN 12,27 AT 22
490   VLIN 12,27 AT 23
500   VLIN 13,25 AT 24
510   VLIN 13,25 AT 25
520   VLIN 12,25 AT 26
530   VLIN 12,20 AT 27
540   VLIN 12,19 AT 28
550   VLIN 12,19 AT 29
560   END
```

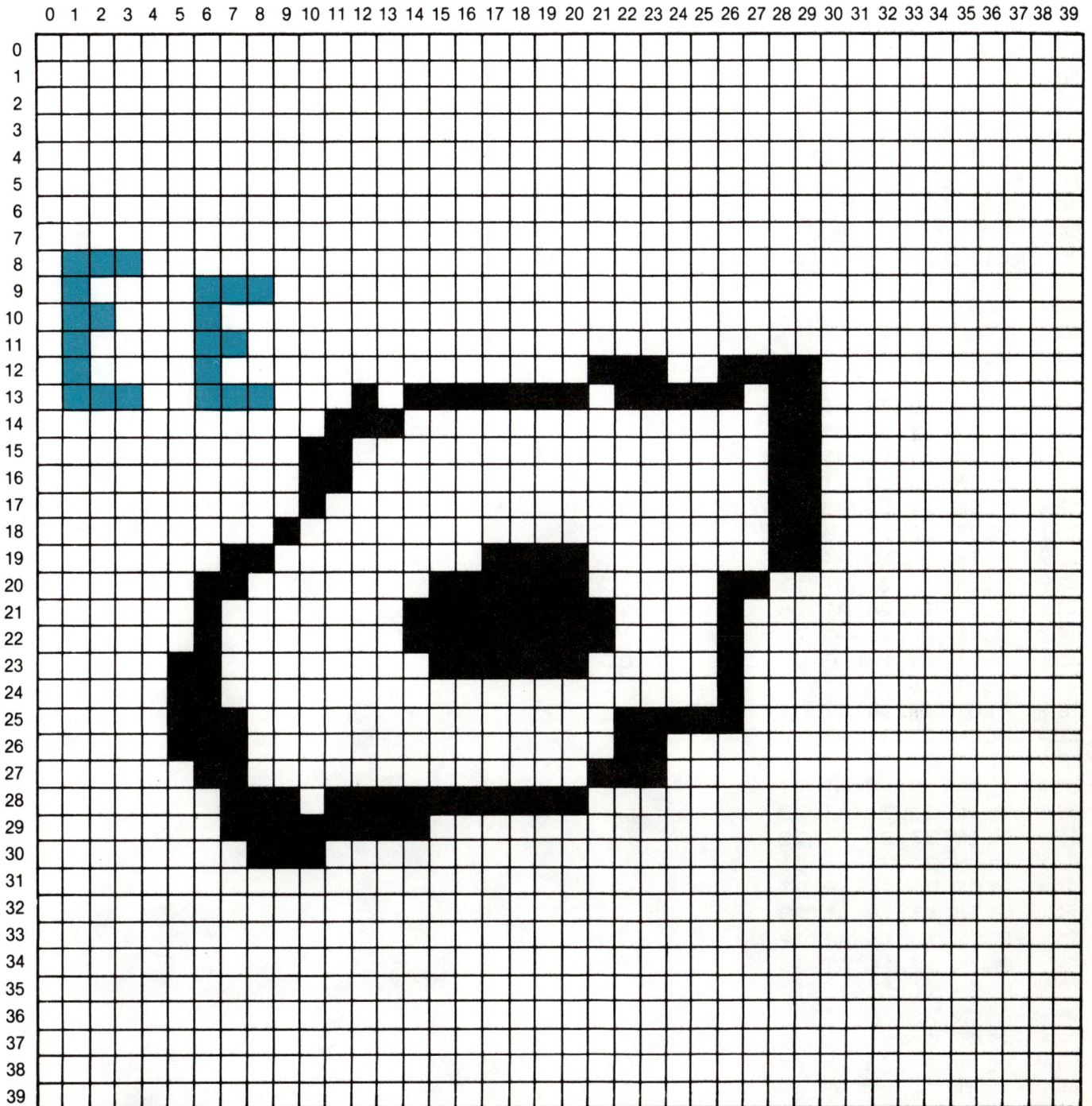

ALTERATIONS:

Eggs need ham or bacon.

What did the egg look like before it was cooked?

Make an Easter egg.

fish

```
10   HOME
20   GR
30   REM   DRAW LARGE F
40   COLOR= 6
50   VLIN 9,13 AT 11
60   HLIN 11,13 AT 8
70   PLOT 12,10
80   REM   DRAW SMALL F
90   VLIN 10,13 AT 16
100  HLIN 16,18 AT 9
110  PLOT 17,11
120  REM   DRAW FISH
130  VLIN 28,29 AT 6
140  PLOT 7,27
150  VLIN 25,26 AT 8
160  VLIN 23,24 AT 9
170  HLIN 10,11 AT 22
180  HLIN 12,13 AT 21
190  HLIN 14,16 AT 20
200  PLOT 17,19
210  HLIN 18,20 AT 18
220  HLIN 21,23 AT 17
230  HLIN 24,26 AT 16
240  VLIN 12,15 AT 25
250  PLOT 26,11: PLOT 27,12: PLOT
     28,13
260  PLOT 29,14
270  HLIN 27,28 AT 15
280  PLOT 25,17
290  VLIN 18,19 AT 24
300  VLIN 20,21 AT 23
310  VLIN 22,23 AT 22
320  VLIN 24,25 AT 21
330  PLOT 20,26: PLOT 19,27
340  HLIN 17,18 AT 28
350  HLIN 15,16 AT 29
360  HLIN 12,14 AT 30
370  HLIN 9,11 AT 31
380  HLIN 7,8 AT 30
390  REM   DRAW FIN
400  VLIN 23,25 AT 17
410  PLOT 16,25
420  HLIN 14,16 AT 26
430  REM   DRAW EYE
440  COLOR= 8
450  PLOT 9,28
460  END
```

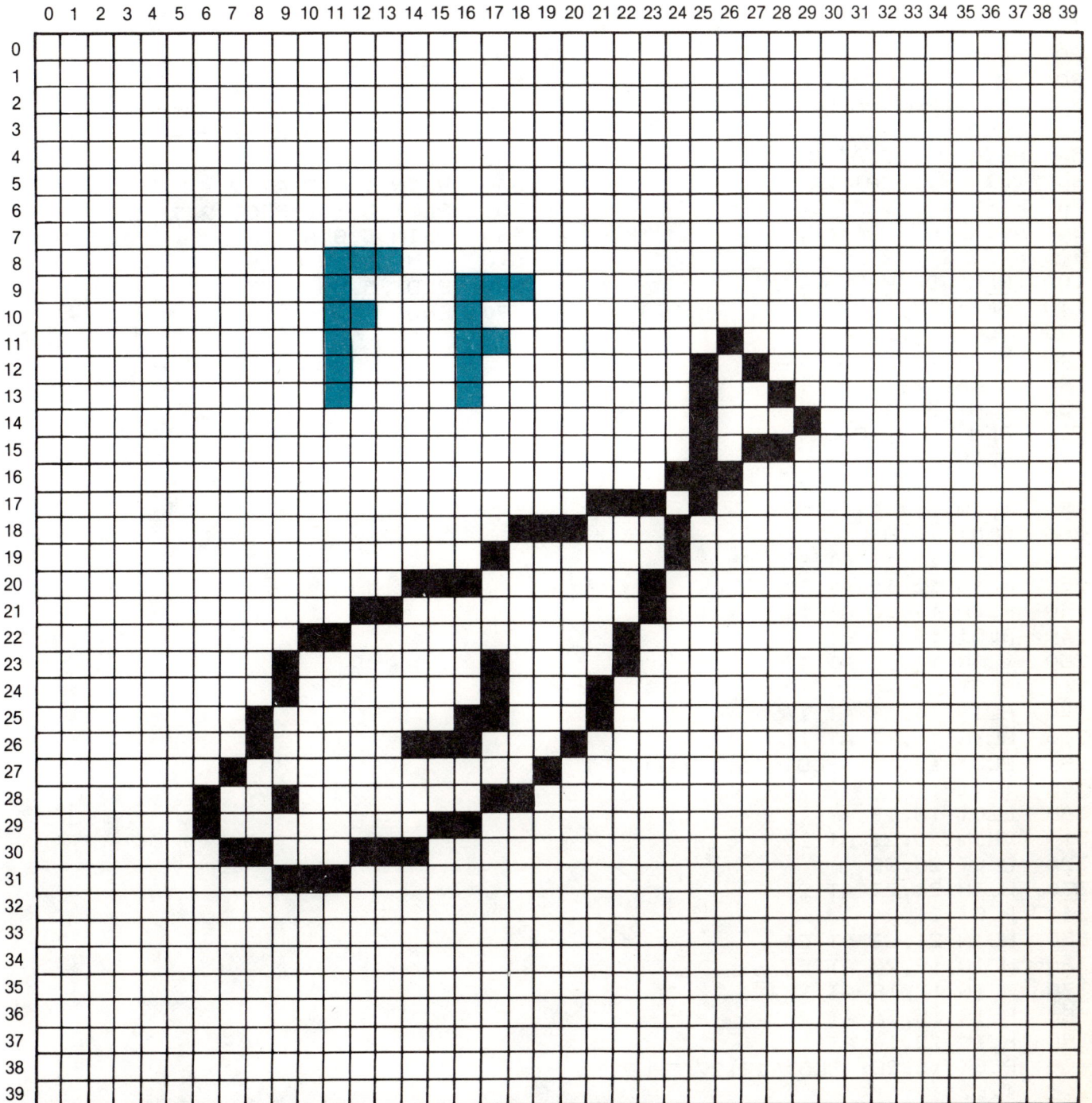

0 1 2 3 4 5 6 7 8 9 10 11 12 13 14 15 16 17 18 19 20 21 22 23 24 25 26 27 28 29 30 31 32 33 34 35 36 37 38 39

ALTERATIONS:

Add blue and gray scales to fish.
Add seaweed.
Add two smaller fish.

Do you see a large shark sneaking up behind the fish? JAWS???????

ghost

```
10    HOME
20    GR
30    REM   DRAW LARGE G
40    COLOR= 5
50    HLIN 21,23 AT 8
60    VLIN 9,13 AT 21
70    HLIN 22,23 AT 13
80    VLIN 10,12 AT 23
90    PLOT 24,10
100   REM   DRAW SMALL G
110   HLIN 27,29 AT 9
120   VLIN 10,13 AT 27
130   HLIN 28,29 AT 13
140   VLIN 11,12 AT 29
150   PLOT 30,11
160   REM   DRAW GHOST
170   HLIN 4,7 AT 4
180   PLOT 8,5
190   VLIN 6,7 AT 9
200   PLOT 10,8
210   HLIN 10,11 AT 9
220   HLIN 12,14 AT 10
230   HLIN 15,18 AT 11
240   PLOT 18,12
250   VLIN 13,14 AT 19
260   PLOT 20,15
270   HLIN 18,19 AT 16
280   HLIN 15,17 AT 15
290   PLOT 15,16: PLOT 16,17: PLOT
      17,18
300   PLOT 18,19
310   VLIN 20,21 AT 19
320   PLOT 20,22
330   HLIN 21,22 AT 23
340   PLOT 23,24
350   HLIN 21,22 AT 25
360   HLIN 19,20 AT 26
370   HLIN 17,18 AT 27
380   HLIN 15,16 AT 28
390   HLIN 12,14 AT 29
400   PLOT 12,28: PLOT 13,27: PLOT
      12,26
410   PLOT 13,25: PLOT 12,24: PLOT
      13,23
420   VLIN 21,22 AT 12
430   HLIN 10,11 AT 20
440   HLIN 9,10 AT 19
450   HLIN 7,8 AT 20
460   PLOT 6,21: PLOT 5,22
470   PLOT 4,23: PLOT 3,24
480   VLIN 22,23 AT 2
490   VLIN 20,21 AT 1
500   VLIN 18,19 AT 2
510   VLIN 15,17 AT 3
520   VLIN 13,14 AT 4
530   PLOT 3,13
540   VLIN 11,12 AT 2
550   PLOT 3,10: PLOT 2,9
560   VLIN 5,8 AT 3
570   REM   DRAW EYES
580   PLOT 5,8: PLOT 7,7
590   END
```

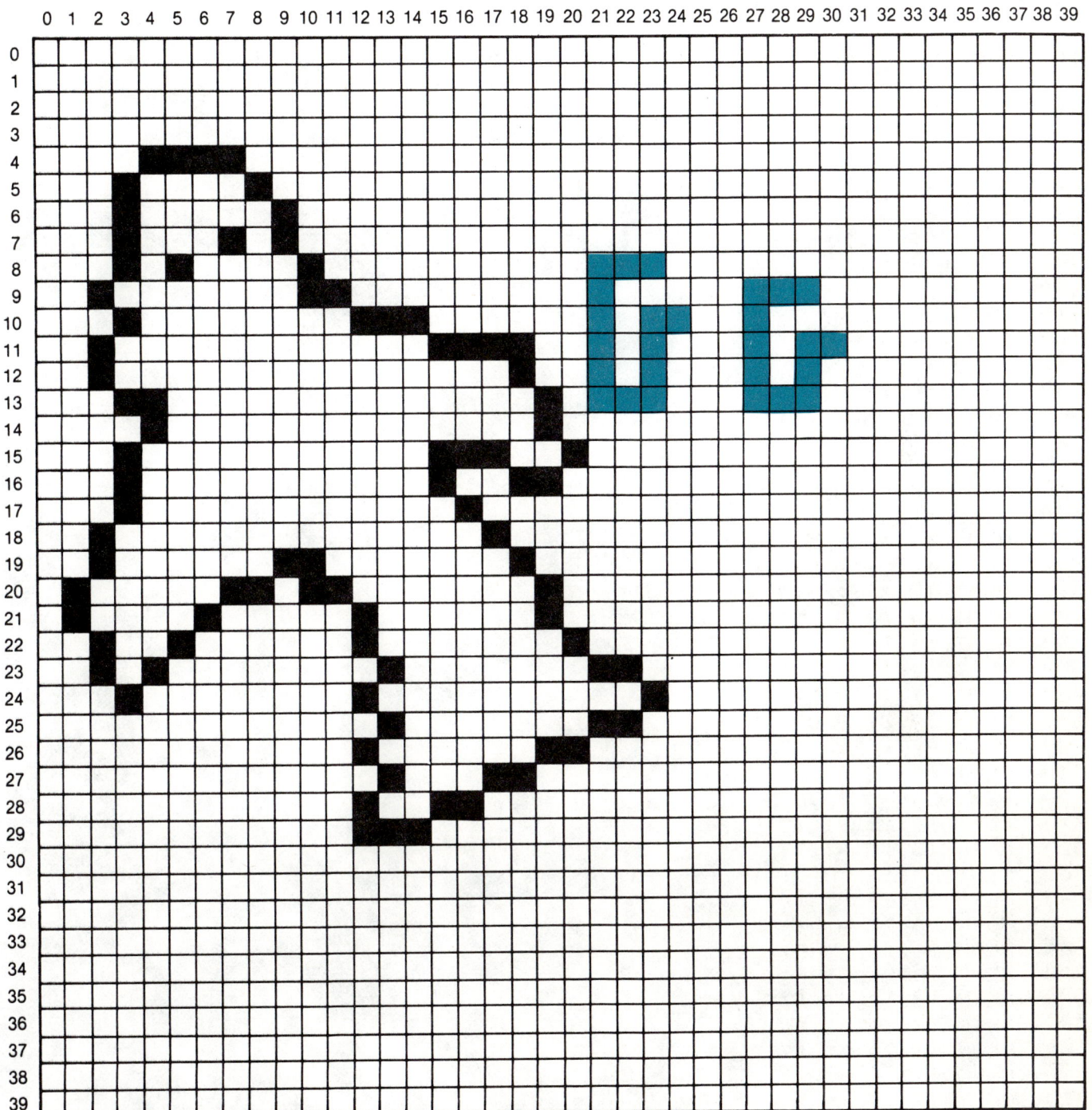

ALTERATIONS:
Every ghost needs a jack-o-lantern.
Will your ghost say BOOO or OOOOOO?
Does your ghost have a smile?
Or does he have sharp white teeth?

Add g words:

Go! Gray ghost!!

house

```
10    HOME
20    GR
30    REM   DRAW BIG H
40    COLOR= 6
50    VLIN 8,13 AT 33
60    VLIN 8,13 AT 35
70    VLIN 10,11 AT 34
80    REM   DRAW SMALL H
90    VLIN 9,13 AT 37
100   PLOT 38,11
110   VLIN 11,13 AT 39
120   REM   DRAW HOUSE
130   COLOR= 1
140   HLIN 10,25 AT 9
150   HLIN 10,25 AT 21
160   VLIN 10,20 AT 10
170   VLIN 10,20 AT 25
180   REM   DRAW ROOF
190   COLOR= 8
200   PLOT 17,1: PLOT 18,1
210   PLOT 16,2: PLOT 19,2
220   PLOT 15,3: PLOT 20,3
230   PLOT 14,4: PLOT 21,4
240   PLOT 13,5: PLOT 22,5
250   PLOT 12,6: PLOT 23,6
260   PLOT 11,7: PLOT 24,7
270   PLOT 10,8: PLOT 25,8
280   PLOT 9,9: PLOT 26,9
290   PLOT 8,10: PLOT 27,10
300   REM   DRAW WINDOWS
310   HLIN 13,15 AT 12
320   HLIN 13,15 AT 14
330   PLOT 13,13: PLOT 15,13
340   HLIN 20,22 AT 12
350   HLIN 20,22 AT 14
360   PLOT 20,13: PLOT 22,13
370   REM   DRAW DOOR
380   HLIN 16,19 AT 17
390   VLIN 18,20 AT 16
400   VLIN 18,20 AT 19
410   COLOR= 7
420   PLOT 17,19
430   END
```

ALTERATIONS:

Add a chimney.
Add lights to the window.
Add a tree and flowers.
Add a sidewalk.
Add a stream flowing gently by.

ink

```
10    HOME
20    GR
30    REM   DRAW BIG I
40    COLOR= 15
50    VLIN 17,20 AT 2
60    HLIN 1,3 AT 16
70    HLIN 1,3 AT 21
80    REM   DRAW SMALL I
90    VLIN 19,21 AT 6
100   PLOT 6,17
110   REM   DRAW WORD INK
120   VLIN 16,25 AT 15
130   VLIN 16,25 AT 17
140   VLIN 18,20 AT 18
150   VLIN 21,23 AT 19
160   VLIN 16,25 AT 20
170   VLIN 16,25 AT 22
180   PLOT 23,20: PLOT 24,19: PLOT
      24,21
190   VLIN 16,18 AT 25
200   VLIN 22,25 AT 25
210   REM   DRAW BOTTLE
220   COLOR= 14
230   VLIN 13,31 AT 12
240   HLIN 13,27 AT 13
250   VLIN 13,31 AT 28
260   HLIN 13,27 AT 31
270   HLIN 13,27 AT 28
280   VLIN 10,12 AT 14
290   VLIN 10,12 AT 15
300   VLIN 10,12 AT 25
310   VLIN 10,12 AT 26
320   HLIN 16,24 AT 10
330   HLIN 16,24 AT 11
340   END
```

ALTERATIONS:

What color is the ink in the bottle? Change the color of the word
ink so that it is that color.
Make the bottle taller.
Can you add a pen?

jack-o-lantern

```
10    HOME
20    GR
30    REM   DRAW BIG J
40    COLOR= 12
50    VLIN 16,21 AT 11
60    PLOT 10,21
70    VLIN 20,21 AT 9
80    REM   DRAW SMALL J
90    VLIN 17,21 AT 16
100   PLOT 15,21
110   VLIN 20,21 AT 14
120   REM   DRAW PUMPKIN STEM
130   COLOR= 8
140   VLIN 14,15 AT 27
150   PLOT 28,15
160   REM   DRAW JACK
170   COLOR= 9
180   HLIN 25,29 AT 16
190   HLIN 23,24 AT 17
200   HLIN 30,31 AT 17
210   PLOT 26,17: PLOT 28,17
220   PLOT 23,18: PLOT 29,18: PLOT
      31,18
230   VLIN 18,19 AT 25
240   VLIN 18,20 AT 27
250   VLIN 19,20 AT 21
260   PLOT 22,19: PLOT 32,19
270   VLIN 19,20 AT 30
280   VLIN 20,21 AT 31
290   VLIN 19,20 AT 33
300   VLIN 20,21 AT 34
310   PLOT 23,21: PLOT 26,21: PLOT
      24,20
320   VLIN 20,21 AT 20
330   PLOT 35,21
340   PLOT 19,22: PLOT 22,22: PLOT
      25,22
350   PLOT 32,22: PLOT 36,22
360   PLOT 18,23: PLOT 37,23
370   HLIN 20,35 AT 23
380   VLIN 24,36 AT 38
390   PLOT 37,37: PLOT 36,38
400   HLIN 20,35 AT 39
410   PLOT 18,37
420   PLOT 19,38
430   VLIN 24,36 AT 17
440   REM   DRAW EYES
450   PLOT 21,26: PLOT 23,25
460   PLOT 23,27
470   VLIN 26,27 AT 22
480   VLIN 26,27 AT 24
490   PLOT 31,25: PLOT 30,26
500   HLIN 32,33 AT 26
510   HLIN 30,32 AT 27
520   REM   DRAW NOSE
530   PLOT 27,29: PLOT 26,30
540   PLOT 27,31: PLOT 28,30
550   REM   DRAW MOUTH
560   HLIN 22,32 AT 33
570   PLOT 33,32
580   VLIN 32,35 AT 34
590   PLOT 32,34: PLOT 33,36: PLOT
      32,36
600   HLIN 24,32 AT 37
610   HLIN 28,29 AT 34
620   HLIN 28,29 AT 36
630   HLIN 25,26 AT 36
640   HLIN 24,25 AT 34
650   VLIN 36,37 AT 23
660   PLOT 22,35
670   VLIN 32,34 AT 21
680   END
```

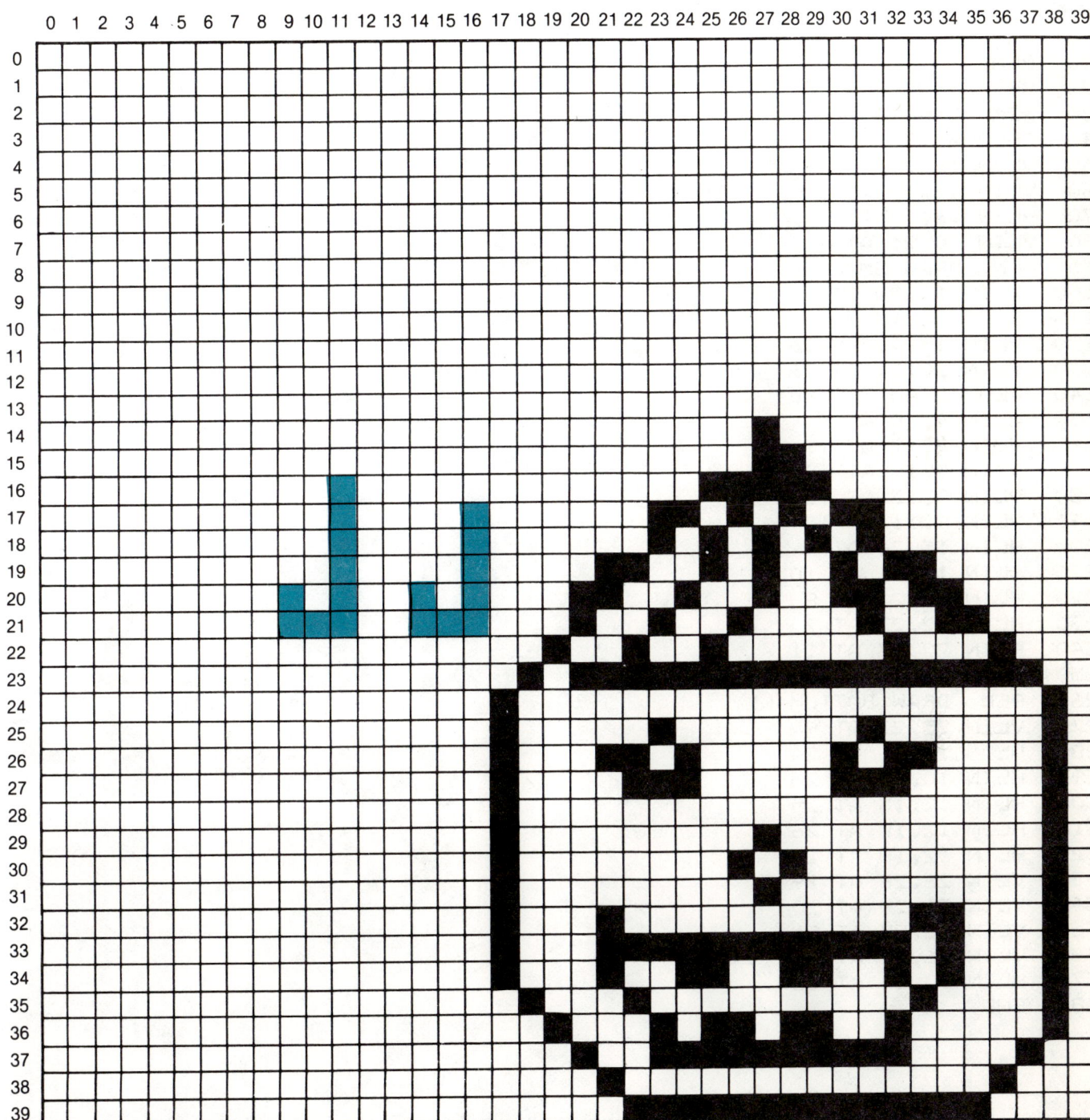

ALTERATIONS:
Make the jack-o-lantern's eyes light up.
Add a witch's face.
Add the word Halloween.
Add the date Oct. 31st

keys

```
10   HOME
20   GR
30   REM   DRAW BIG K
40   COLOR= 13
50   VLIN 16,21 AT 19
60   VLIN 18,19 AT 20
70   VLIN 16,17 AT 21
80   VLIN 20,21 AT 21
90   REM   DRAW SMALL K
100   VLIN 17,21 AT 24
110   PLOT 25,19
120   VLIN 17,18 AT 26
130   VLIN 20,21 AT 26
140   REM   DRAW TOP KEY
150   HLIN 9,10 AT 9
160   VLIN 9,12 AT 11
170   VLIN 9,10 AT 12
180   VLIN 9,12 AT 13
190   VLIN 9,11 AT 14
200   HLIN 15,21 AT 9
210   HLIN 15,21 AT 10
220   HLIN 20,21 AT 8
230   HLIN 22,23 AT 7
240   HLIN 22,23 AT 11
250   VLIN 8,10 AT 24
260   REM   DRAW BOTTOM KEY
270   VLIN 25,27 AT 9
280   HLIN 10,11 AT 24
290   HLIN 10,11 AT 28
300   HLIN 12,13 AT 25
310   HLIN 12,18 AT 26
320   HLIN 12,18 AT 27
330   VLIN 26,28 AT 19
340   VLIN 26,29 AT 20
350   VLIN 26,27 AT 21
360   VLIN 26,29 AT 22
370   HLIN 23,24 AT 26
380   END
```

ALTERATIONS:
Add a keyhole for each key.
Add a different kind of key.
What key do you sing in? Add the bass or treble sign.
Add an old fashioned lock.

lamp

```
10    HOME
20    GR
30    REM   DRAW BIG L
40    COLOR= 4
50    VLIN 16,21 AT 29
60    HLIN 30,31 AT 21
70    REM   DRAW SMALL L
80    VLIN 17,21 AT 34
90    HLIN 35,36 AT 21
100   REM   DRAW LAMP
110   COLOR= 2
120   HLIN 13,18 AT 3
130   PLOT 12,4: PLOT 19,4
140   PLOT 11,5: PLOT 20,5
150   PLOT 10,6: PLOT 21,6
160   PLOT 9,7: PLOT 22,7
170   PLOT 8,8: PLOT 23,8
180   PLOT 7,9: PLOT 24,9
190   PLOT 6,10: PLOT 8,10: PLOT 1
      0,10
200   PLOT 12,10: PLOT 14,10: PLOT
      16,10
210   PLOT 18,10: PLOT 20,10: PLOT
      22,10
220   HLIN 24,25 AT 10
230   PLOT 7,11: PLOT 9,11: PLOT 1
      1,11
240   PLOT 13,11: PLOT 15,11: PLOT
      17,11
250   PLOT 19,11: PLOT 21,11: PLOT
      23,11
260   VLIN 12,21 AT 16
270   HLIN 10,22 AT 22
280   HLIN 10,22 AT 26
290   VLIN 23,25 AT 10
300   VLIN 23,25 AT 22
310   END
```

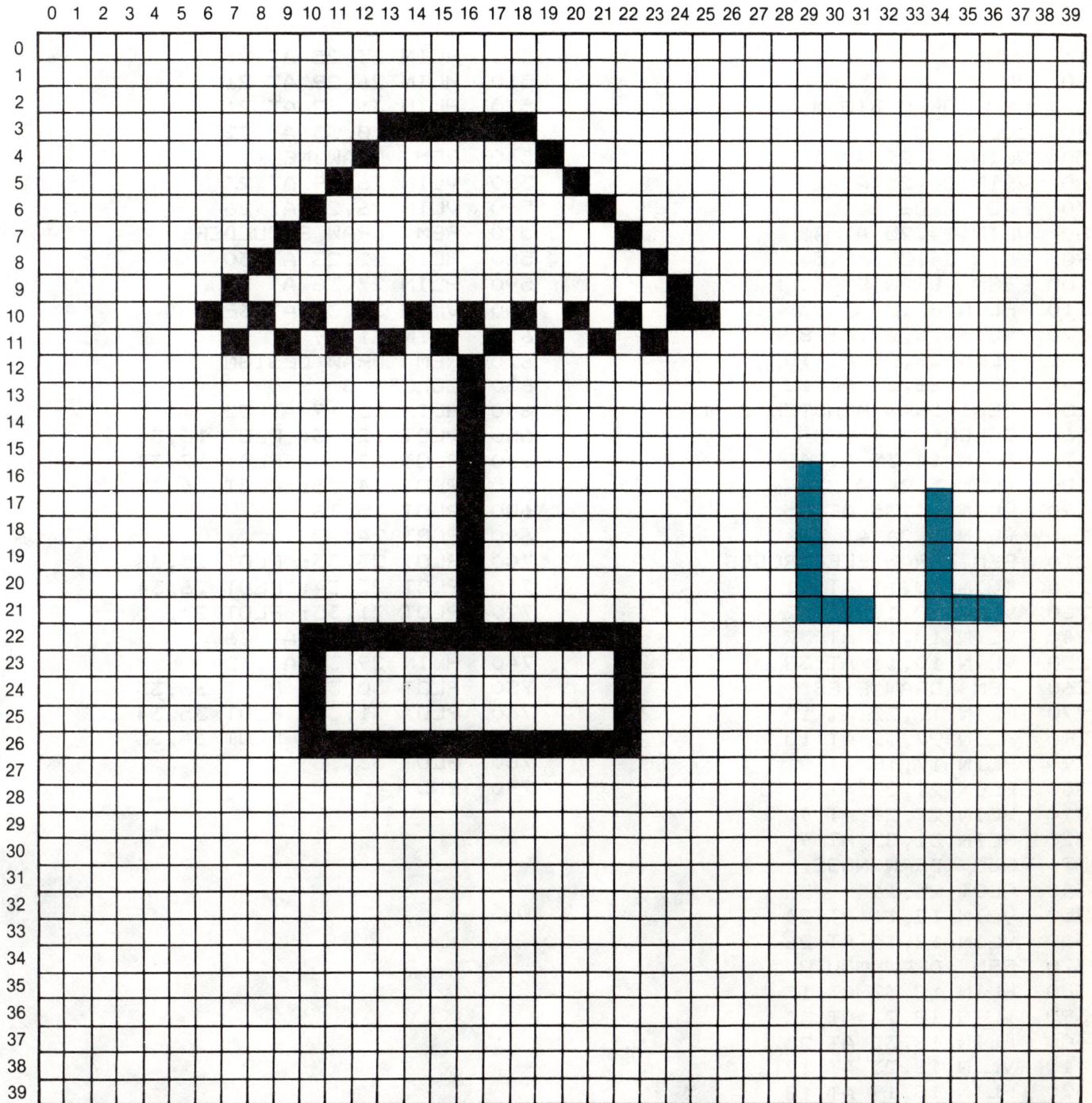

ALTERATIONS:
How many "L" words can you add?
Lovely lamps light lively living rooms.

monster

```
10    HOME
20    GR
30    REM   DRAW BIG M
40    COLOR= 5
50    VLIN 24,29 AT 1
60    VLIN 24,25 AT 2
70    PLOT 3,26
80    VLIN 24,25 AT 4
90    VLIN 24,29 AT 5
100   REM   DRAW SMALL M
110   HLIN 8,12 AT 25
120   VLIN 26,29 AT 8
130   VLIN 26,29 AT 10
140   VLIN 26,29 AT 12
150   REM   DRAW MONSTER'S HEAD
160   COLOR= 4
170   HLIN 14,35 AT 4
180   VLIN 5,24 AT 36
190   HLIN 14,35 AT 25
200   VLIN 5,24 AT 13
210   REM   DRAW ELECTRODES
220   VLIN 10,11 AT 11
230   VLIN 10,11 AT 12
240   VLIN 10,11 AT 37
250   VLIN 10,11 AT 38
260   REM   DRAW EYES
270   HLIN 17,22 AT 10
280   HLIN 27,32 AT 10
290   HLIN 17,18 AT 9
300   HLIN 21,22 AT 9
310   HLIN 27,28 AT 9
320   HLIN 31,32 AT 9
330   REM   DRAW NOSE
340   PLOT 25,14
350   VLIN 12,14 AT 24
360   VLIN 12,14 AT 26
370   REM   DRAW MOUTH
380   HLIN 18,32 AT 17
390   VLIN 18,22 AT 33
400   HLIN 18,32 AT 23
410   VLIN 18,23 AT 17
420   HLIN 18,19 AT 18
430   HLIN 21,23 AT 18
440   HLIN 25,27 AT 18
450   HLIN 29,31 AT 18
460   PLOT 18,19: PLOT 22,19: PLOT
      26,19
470   PLOT 30,19: PLOT 32,20
480   PLOT 28,20: PLOT 24,20: PLOT
      20,20
490   HLIN 19,21 AT 21
500   HLIN 23,25 AT 21
510   HLIN 26,29 AT 21
520   HLIN 31,32 AT 21
530   HLIN 18,33 AT 22
540   REM   DRAW NECK
550   VLIN 26,29 AT 23
560   VLIN 26,29 AT 26
570   REM   DRAW SHOULDERS
580   HLIN 12,23 AT 30
590   HLIN 27,38 AT 30
600   VLIN 31,39 AT 38
610   VLIN 31,39 AT 11
620   REM   DRAW DESIGN
630   COLOR= 8
640   HLIN 12,19 AT 32
650   PLOT 12,33: PLOT 18,33
660   PLOT 13,34: PLOT 17,34
670   PLOT 14,35: PLOT 16,35
680   PLOT 15,36
690   PLOT 24,32
700   PLOT 23,33: PLOT 25,33
710   PLOT 22,34: PLOT 26,34
720   PLOT 21,35: PLOT 27,35
730   HLIN 20,28 AT 36
740   HLIN 29,37 AT 32
750   PLOT 30,33: PLOT 36,33
760   PLOT 31,34: PLOT 35,34
770   PLOT 32,35: PLOT 34,35
780   PLOT 33,36
790   END
```

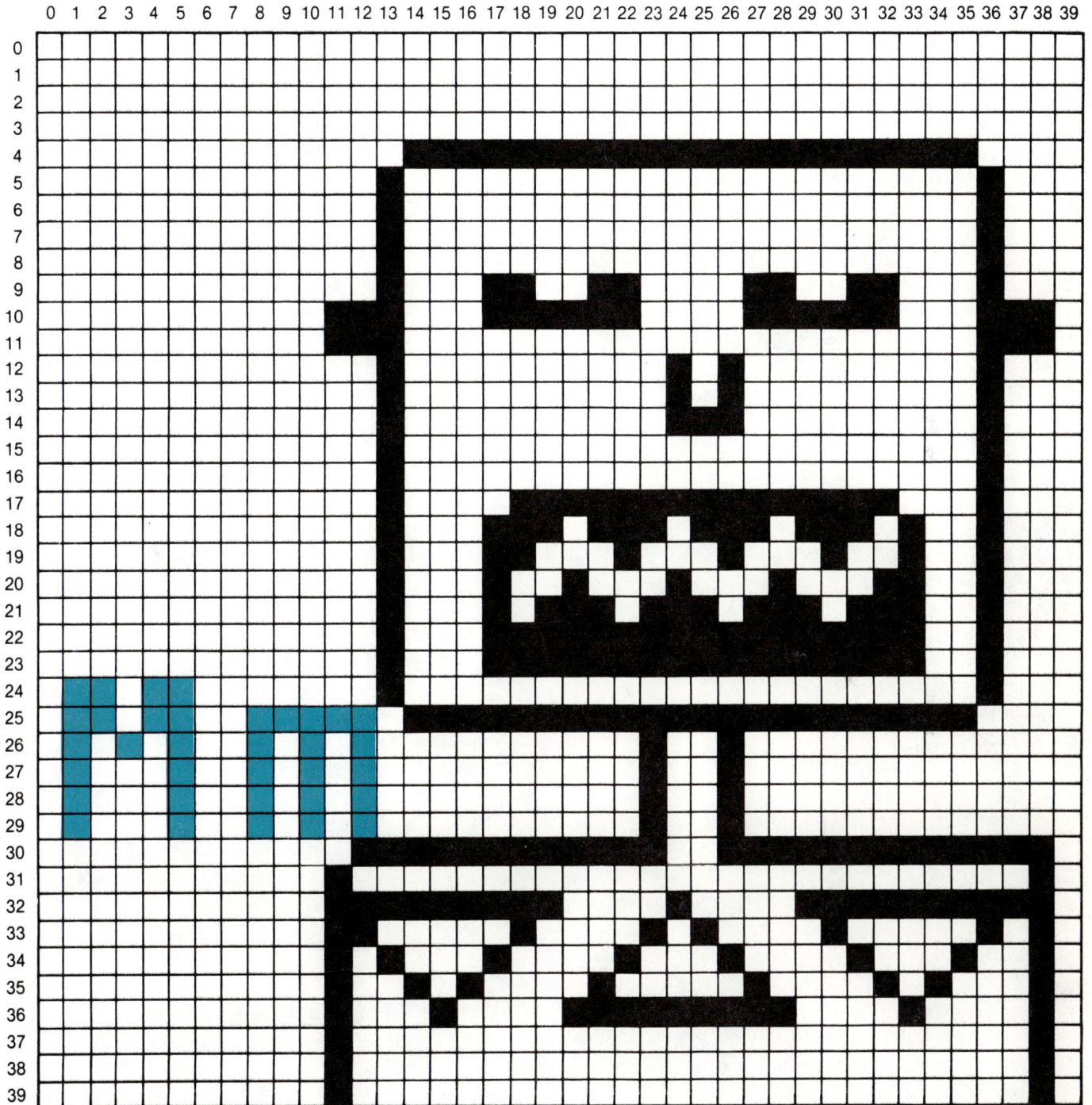

ALTERATIONS:

This is my monster!! Can you make one of your own?
I'll bet yours is even uglier than mine

Finished with Chapter 5
ALREADY???
GREAT!!!

Save some of the following programs until you have read
Chapters 7 and 8.

Activity units
N–Z
6

NAME (YOURS)
OWL
PIANO
ROCKET
SQUIRREL
TOTEM
UFO
VIOLETS
WATERMELON SLICE
XANADU
YOUR FAVORITE THING
ZIPPER

name

```
10    HOME
20    GR
30    REM   DRAW LARGE N
40    COLOR= 9
50    VLIN 24,29 AT 15
60    VLIN 24,25 AT 16
70    VLIN 26,27 AT 17
80    VLIN 24,29 AT 18
90    REM   DRAW SMALL N
100   VLIN 25,29 AT 21
110   PLOT 22,26
120   VLIN 26,29 AT 23
130   END
```

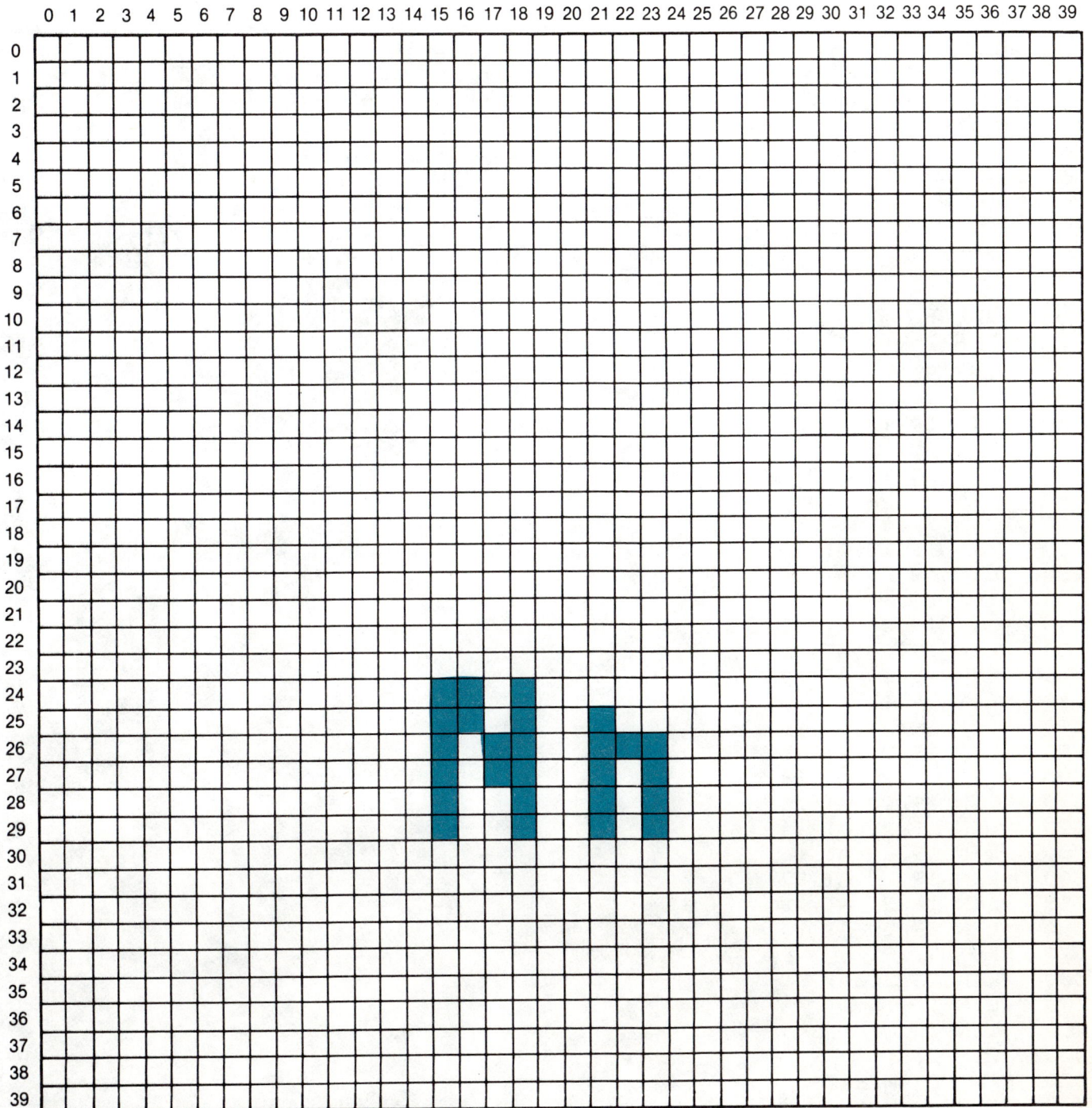

ALTERATIONS:

N is for Name. I left this sheet blank for you to design your own
name screen. Be fancy. It's all for you!!

owl

```
10    HOME
20    GR
30    REM   DRAW BIG O
40    COLOR= 9
50    VLIN 24,29 AT 26
60    VLIN 24,29 AT 28
70    PLOT 27,24: PLOT 27,29
80    REM   DRAW SMALL O
90    VLIN 25,29 AT 31
100   VLIN 25,29 AT 33
110   PLOT 32,25: PLOT 32,29
120   REM   DRAW OWL'S HEAD
130   COLOR= 8
140   PLOT 8,1: PLOT 9,2
150   HLIN 10,13 AT 3
160   HLIN 14,17 AT 2
170   HLIN 18,22 AT 3
180   PLOT 23,2: PLOT 24,1
190   VLIN 2,3 AT 25
200   VLIN 3,16 AT 26
210   VLIN 17,18 AT 25
220   VLIN 18,20 AT 24
230   PLOT 23,19
240   VLIN 19,20 AT 22
250   VLIN 19,20 AT 21
260   VLIN 19,20 AT 20
270   VLIN 19,22 AT 19
280   VLIN 19,20 AT 18
290   VLIN 19,20 AT 17
300   VLIN 19,20 AT 16
310   VLIN 19,20 AT 15
320   VLIN 19,21 AT 14
330   VLIN 19,20 AT 13
340   VLIN 19,20 AT 12
350   VLIN 19,21 AT 11
360   VLIN 19,20 AT 10
370   PLOT 9,19
380   VLIN 18,20 AT 8
390   VLIN 17,18 AT 7
400   VLIN 3,16 AT 6
410   VLIN 2,3 AT 7
420   REM   DRAW EYES
430   COLOR= 15
440   VLIN 8,11 AT 12
450   VLIN 8,11 AT 18
460   PLOT 13,8: PLOT 13,11
470   PLOT 19,8: PLOT 19,11
480   COLOR= 8
490   VLIN 7,12 AT 11
500   VLIN 7,12 AT 14
510   HLIN 12,13 AT 7
520   HLIN 12,13 AT 12
530   VLIN 7,12 AT 17
540   VLIN 7,12 AT 20
550   HLIN 18,19 AT 7
560   HLIN 18,19 AT 12
570   REM   DRAW BEAK
580   HLIN 13,17 AT 14
590   PLOT 13,15: PLOT 17,15
600   HLIN 14,16 AT 16
610   PLOT 15,17
620   END
```

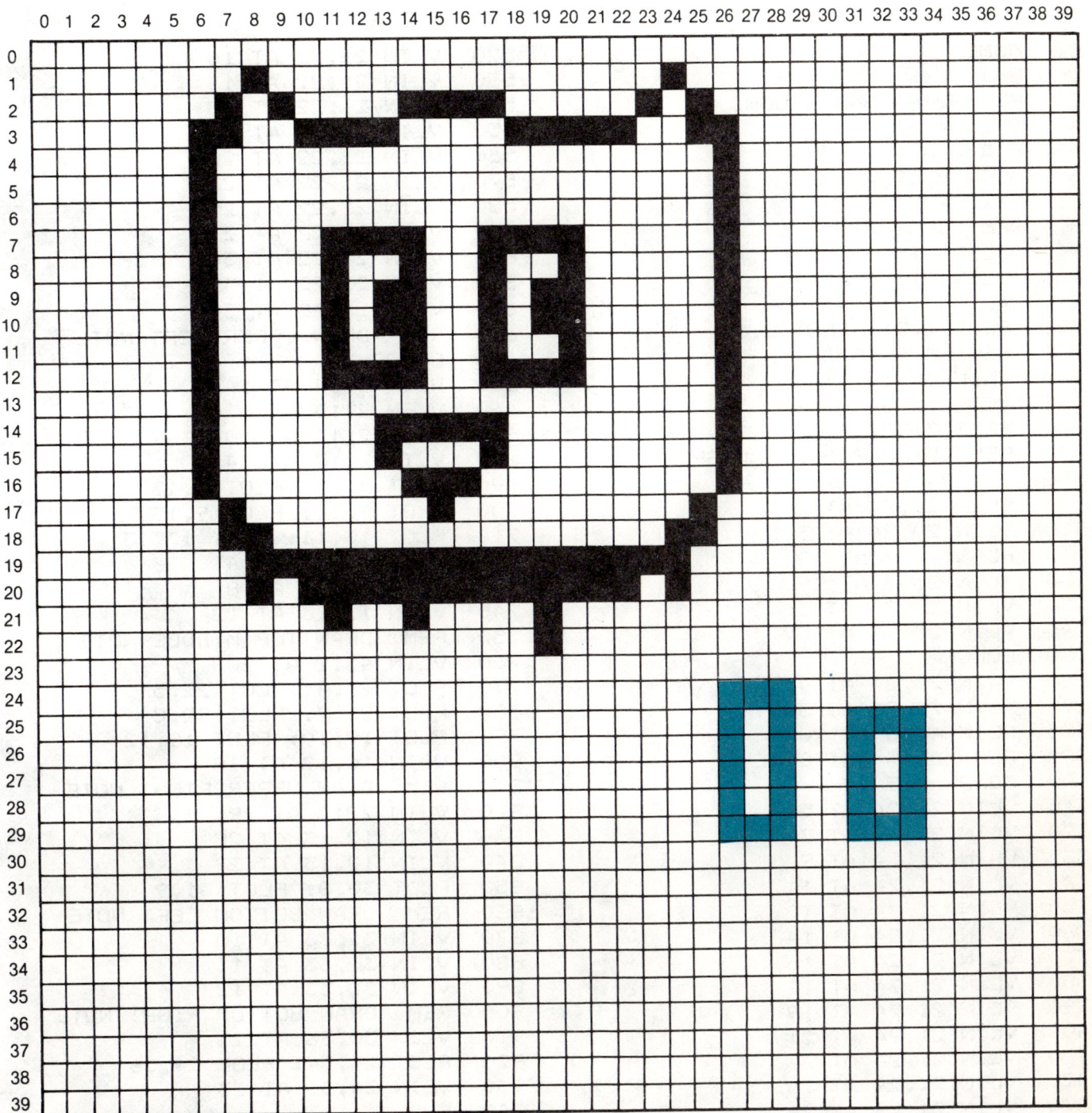

ALTERATIONS:
Make the owl's eyes blink—hint change the color.
Add the owl's body.
Add a tree limb for him to sit on.

piano

```
10    HOME
20    GR
30    REM   DRAW BACKGROUND
40    COLOR= 7
50    FOR X = 0 TO 39
60    HLIN 0,39 AT X
70    NEXT X
80    REM   DRAW BIG P
90    COLOR= 15
100   VLIN 31,36 AT 1
110   VLIN 31,33 AT 3
120   PLOT 2,31: PLOT 2,33
130   REM   DRAW SMALL P
140   VLIN 32,36 AT 6
150   VLIN 32,34 AT 8
160   PLOT 7,32: PLOT 7,34
170   REM   DRAW PIANO BACKGROUND
180   COLOR= 8
190   VLIN 20,24 AT 2
200   VLIN 20,24 AT 3
210   HLIN 2,37 AT 18
220   HLIN 2,37 AT 19
230   VLIN 20,24 AT 36
240   VLIN 20,24 AT 37
250   COLOR= 5
260   VLIN 21,24 AT 4
270   VLIN 21,24 AT 35
280   HLIN 4,35 AT 20
290   REM   DRAW WHITE KEYS
300   COLOR= 15
310   VLIN 21,24 AT 5
320   VLIN 21,24 AT 7
330   VLIN 21,24 AT 9
340   VLIN 21,24 AT 11
350   VLIN 21,24 AT 12
360   VLIN 21,24 AT 14
370   VLIN 21,24 AT 16
380   VLIN 21,24 AT 17
390   VLIN 21,24 AT 19
400   VLIN 21,24 AT 21
410   VLIN 21,24 AT 23
420   VLIN 21,24 AT 24
430   VLIN 21,24 AT 26
440   VLIN 21,24 AT 28
450   VLIN 21,24 AT 29
460   VLIN 21,24 AT 31
470   VLIN 21,24 AT 33
480   REM   DRAW BLACK KEYS
490   COLOR= 0
500   VLIN 21,22 AT 6
510   VLIN 21,22 AT 8
520   VLIN 21,22 AT 10
530   VLIN 21,22 AT 13
540   VLIN 21,22 AT 15
550   VLIN 21,22 AT 18
560   VLIN 21,22 AT 20
570   VLIN 21,22 AT 22
580   VLIN 21,22 AT 25
590   VLIN 21,22 AT 27
600   VLIN 21,22 AT 30
610   VLIN 21,22 AT 32
620   VLIN 21,22 AT 34
630   REM   DRAW UPPER LEFT NOTE
640   COLOR= 2
650   HLIN 6,14 AT 1
660   VLIN 2,13 AT 6
670   VLIN 2,13 AT 10
680   VLIN 2,13 AT 14
690   PLOT 5,11: PLOT 5,13
700   PLOT 9,11: PLOT 9,13
710   PLOT 13,11: PLOT 13,13
720   VLIN 11,13 AT 4
730   VLIN 11,13 AT 8
740   VLIN 11,13 AT 12
750   REM   DRAW TOP MIDDLE NOTE
760   VLIN 4,12 AT 20
770   PLOT 21,4: PLOT 22,5
780   PLOT 21,7: PLOT 22,8
790   PLOT 19,10: PLOT 19,12
800   VLIN 10,12 AT 18
810   REM   DRAW UPPER RIGHT NOTE
820   VLIN 7,13 AT 29
830   VLIN 12,13 AT 28
840   VLIN 12,13 AT 27
850   PLOT 30,8: PLOT 31,9
860   REM   DRAW BOTTOM LEFT NOTE
870   VLIN 31,33 AT 10
880   VLIN 31,33 AT 11
890   VLIN 31,33 AT 12
900   REM   DRAW BOTTOM RIGHT NOTE
910   VLIN 30,36 AT 25
920   PLOT 24,34: PLOT 24,36
930   VLIN 34,36 AT 23
940   END
```

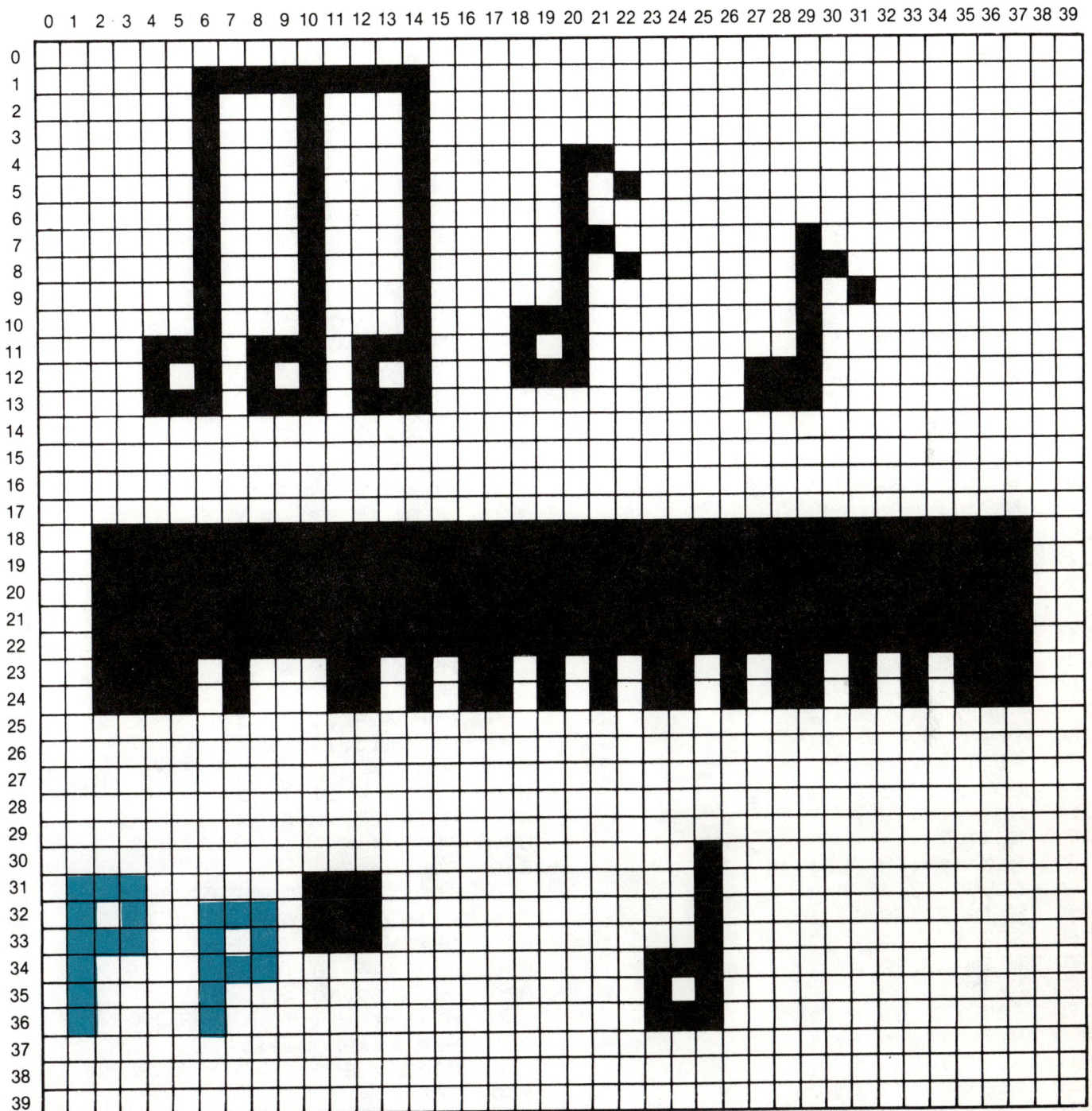

ALTERATIONS:

Make all the notes different colors.

Add more notes.

Add sound when the notes appear.

quilt

```
10    HOME                           520    FOR X = 0 TO 13
20    GR                             530    VLIN 37,39 AT X
30    REM   DRAW CRAZY QUILT         540    NEXT X
40    COLOR= 1                       550    FOR X = 37 TO 39
50    FOR X = 0 TO 2                 560    VLIN 22,36 AT X
60    HLIN 0,8 AT X                  570    NEXT X
70    NEXT X                         580    FOR X = 3 TO 7
80    FOR X = 15 TO 23               590    HLIN 0,4 AT X
90    VLIN 3,9 AT X                  600    NEXT X
100   NEXT X                         610    FOR X = 10 TO 12
110   FOR X = 35 TO 39               620    HLIN 15,22 AT X
120   VLIN 0,3 AT X                  630    NEXT X
130   NEXT X                         640    FOR X = 18 TO 19
140   FOR X = 31 TO 36               650    VLIN 13,20 AT X
150   HLIN 17,24 AT 31               660    NEXT X
160   NEXT X                         670    REM ****GRAY****
170   FOR X = 29 TO 36               680    COLOR= 5
180   VLIN 22,36 AT X                690    FOR X = 7 TO 15
190   NEXT X                         700    VLIN 15,28 AT X
200   FOR X = 14 TO 20               710    NEXT X
210   VLIN 38,39 AT X                720    FOR X = 0 TO 2
220   NEXT X                         730    HLIN 26,34 AT X
230   COLOR= 2                       740    NEXT X
240   FOR X = 13 TO 30               750    FOR X = 11 TO 17
250   HLIN 5,17 AT X                 760    HLIN 34,39 AT X
260   NEXT X                         770    NEXT X
270   FOR X = 9 TO 14                780    FOR X = 31 TO 37
280   VLIN 3,7 AT X                  790    HLIN 15,16 AT X
290   NEXT X                         800    NEXT X
300   FOR X = 35 TO 37               810    FOR X = 21 TO 24
310   HLIN 17,18 AT X                820    HLIN 25,28 AT X
320   NEXT X                         830    NEXT X
330   REM ****PURPLE****             840    COLOR= 7
340   COLOR= 3                       850    FOR X = 30 TO 33
350   HLIN 23,39 AT 10               860    VLIN 13,15 AT X
360   FOR X = 13 TO 26               870    NEXT X
370   HLIN 20,22 AT X                880    FOR X = 18 TO 24
380   NEXT X                         890    VLIN 29,30 AT X
390   FOR X = 23 TO 26               900    NEXT X
400   VLIN 13,15 AT X                910    REM ***BROWN***
410   NEXT X                         920    COLOR= 8
420   FOR X = 23 TO 25               930    FOR X = 3 TO 7
430   VLIN 18,20 AT X                940    HLIN 5,8 AT X
440   NEXT X                         950    NEXT X
450   FOR X = 31 TO 36               960    FOR X = 0 TO 4
460   HLIN 5,10 AT X                 970    VLIN 13,30 AT X
470   NEXT X                         980    NEXT X
480   FOR X = 20 TO 24               990    FOR X = 3 TO 7
490   VLIN 32,36 AT X                1000   HLIN 5,8 AT X
500   NEXT X                         1010   NEXT X
510   COLOR= 4                       1020   FOR X = 18 TO 19
```

```
1030    VLIN 21,28 AT X
1040    NEXT X
1050    FOR X = 20 TO 22
1060    VLIN 27,28 AT X
1070    NEXT X
1080    FOR X = 23 TO 24
1090    VLIN 21,28 AT X
1100    NEXT X
1110    FOR X = 24 TO 34
1120    VLIN 3,7 AT X
1130    NEXT X
1140    REM  ****ORANGE****
1150    COLOR= 9
1160    FOR X = 29 TO 39
1170    VLIN 18,21 AT X
1180    NEXT X
1190    FOR X = 0 TO 2
1200    HLIN 9,25 AT X
1210    NEXT X
1220    FOR X = 21 TO 24
1230    VLIN 37,39 AT X
1240    NEXT X
1250    FOR X = 4 TO 7
1260    HLIN 35,39 AT X
1270    NEXT X
1280    REM  ****GREEN****
1290    COLOR= 12
1300    FOR X = 24 TO 39
1310    VLIN 8,9 AT X
1320    NEXT X
1330    FOR X = 26 TO 28
1340    VLIN 18,20 AT X
1350    NEXT X
1360    REM  ****YELLOW****
1370    COLOR= 13
1380    FOR X = 0 TO 14
1390    VLIN 8,12 AT X
1400    NEXT X
1410    FOR X = 27 TO 29
1420    VLIN 11,17 AT X
1430    NEXT X
1440    FOR X = 23 TO 33
1450    VLIN 11,12 AT X
1460    NEXT X
1470    FOR X = 23 TO 33
1480    VLIN 16,17 AT X
1490    NEXT X
1500    FOR X = 37 TO 39
1510    HLIN 25,39 AT X
1520    NEXT X
1530    FOR X = 25 TO 28
1540    VLIN 34,36 AT X
1550    NEXT X
1560    REM  ****MAGENTA***
1570    COLOR= 1
1580    FOR X = 9 TO 13
1590    VLIN 18,25 AT X
1600    NEXT X
1610    REM  ****WHITE****
1620    COLOR= 15
1630    FOR X = 25 TO 28
1640    VLIN 25,33 AT X
1650    NEXT X
1660    FOR X = 25 TO 27
1670    HLIN 25,33 AT X
1680    NEXT X
1690    FOR X = 29 TO 33
1700    VLIN 31,33 AT X
1710    NEXT X
1720    PLOT 18,33
1730    VLIN 32,35 AT 12
1740    VLIN 32,34 AT 13
1750    REM  ****LT BLUE****
1760    COLOR= 7
1770    FOR X = 0 TO 4
1780    VLIN 31,36 AT X
1790    NEXT X
1800    END
```

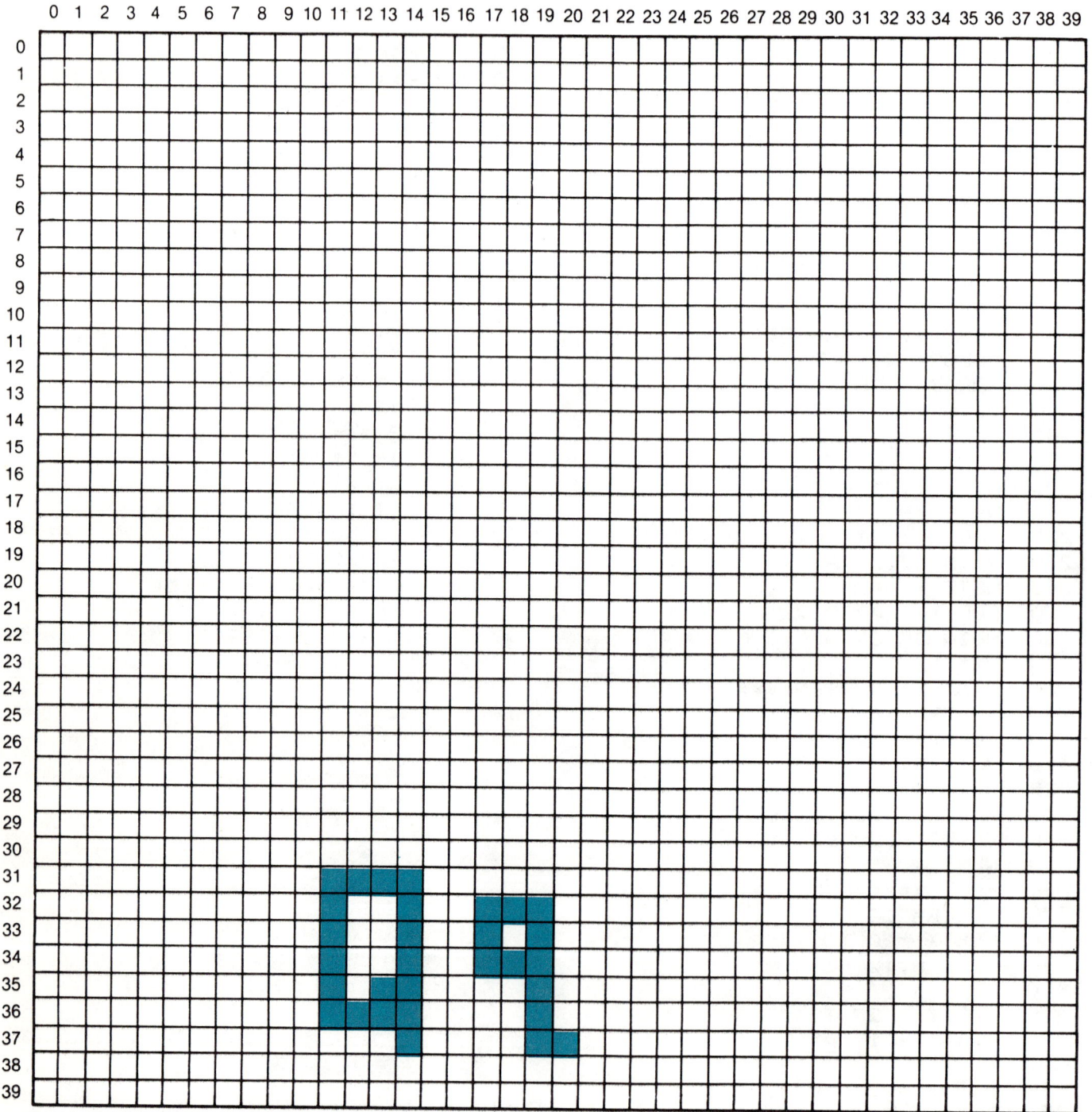

ALTERATIONS:
Design your own quilt.
Make the blocks different colors and sizes.
Add sound when some blocks appear, but not too noisy!

rocket

```
10    HOME
20    GR
30    REM   DRAW BIG R
40    COLOR= 7
50    VLIN 31,36 AT 23
60    HLIN 24,25 AT 31
70    VLIN 32,33 AT 25
80    VLIN 33,34 AT 24
90    VLIN 35,36 AT 25
100   REM   DRAW SMALL R
110   VLIN 32,36 AT 28
120   PLOT 29,33
130   VLIN 33,34 AT 30
140   REM   DRAW ROCKET
150   COLOR= 15
160   VLIN 0,2 AT 10
170   VLIN 3,4 AT 9
180   VLIN 3,4 AT 11
190   VLIN 5,7 AT 8
200   VLIN 5,7 AT 12
210   VLIN 8,37 AT 7
220   VLIN 8,37 AT 13
230   HLIN 8,12 AT 12
240   REM   DRAW LETTERS
250   COLOR= 2
260   VLIN 14,18 AT 9
270   VLIN 21,22 AT 9
280   PLOT 9,25
290   VLIN 28,32 AT 9
300   PLOT 10,18: PLOT 10,21: PLOT
      10,23
310   PLOT 10,25: PLOT 10,28: PLOT
      10,30
320   VLIN 14,18 AT 11
330   PLOT 11,21
340   VLIN 24,25 AT 11
350   VLIN 28,32 AT 11
360   REM   DRAW FINS
370   PLOT 6,26: PLOT 5,27
380   PLOT 14,26: PLOT 15,27
390   VLIN 28,36 AT 4
400   VLIN 28,36 AT 16
410   PLOT 5,35: PLOT 6,36
420   PLOT 15,35: PLOT 14,36
430   REM   DRAW BOOSTER
440   COLOR= 1
450   VLIN 38,39 AT 8
460   VLIN 38,39 AT 9
470   VLIN 38,39 AT 11
480   VLIN 38,39 AT 12
490   END
```

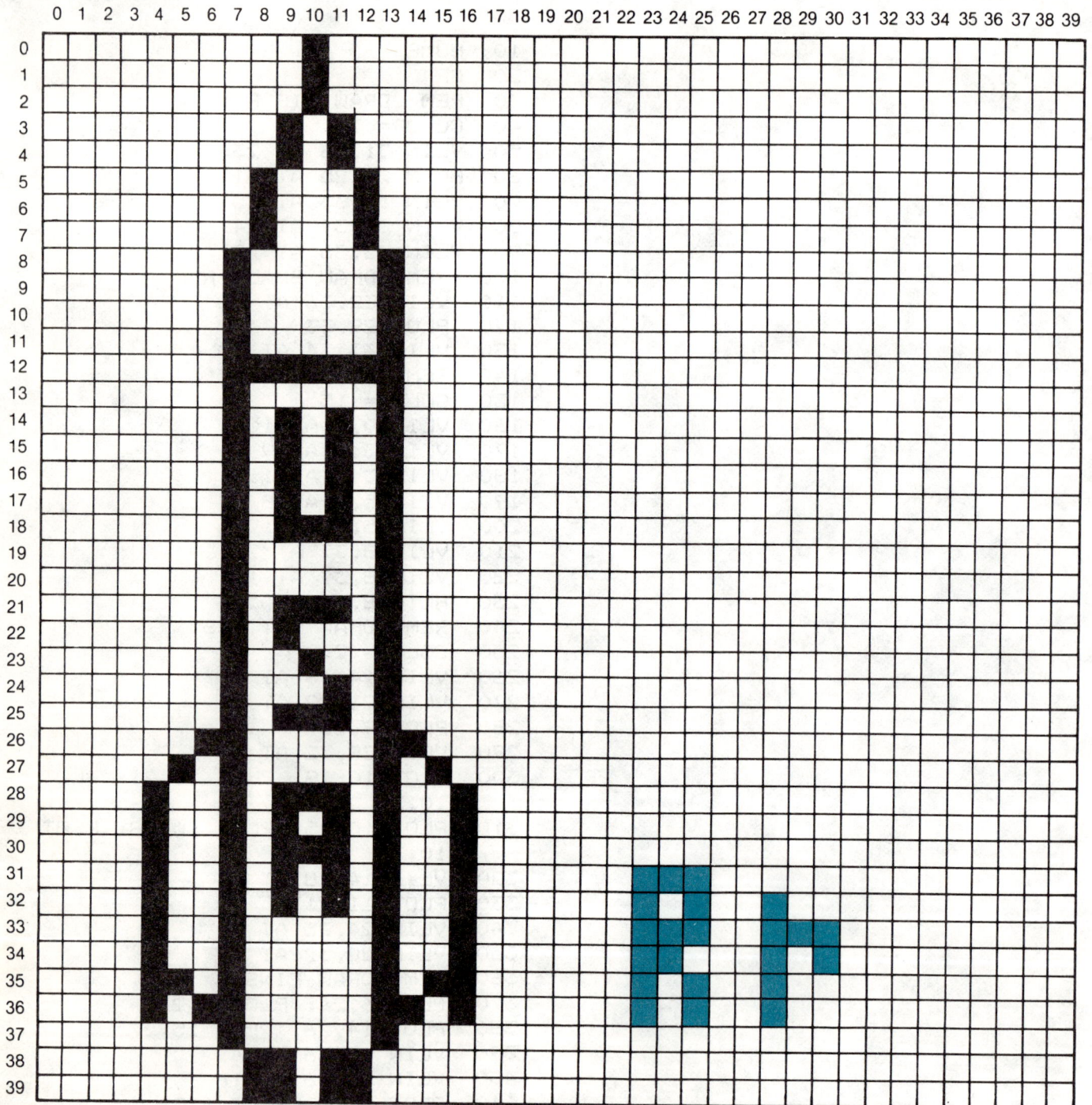

ALTERATIONS:
Fill in the rest of the rocket.
Make the boosters blink.
Add a landscape.
Add a launch tower.

squirrel

```
10   HOME
20   GR
30   REM   DRAW BIG S
40   COLOR= 4
50   HLIN 33,35 AT 31
60   HLIN 33,34 AT 32
70   PLOT 33,33
80   HLIN 34,35 AT 34
90   VLIN 35,36 AT 35
100   HLIN 33,34 AT 36
110   REM   DRAW SMALL S
120   HLIN 38,39 AT 32
130   PLOT 38,33
140   VLIN 34,36 AT 39
150   PLOT 38,36
160   REM   DRAW SQUIRREL'S TAIL
170   COLOR= 8
180   HLIN 5,14 AT 1
190   PLOT 4,2: PLOT 15,2: PLOT 3,
      3
200   HLIN 16,17 AT 3
210   PLOT 2,4: PLOT 18,4
220   VLIN 5,9 AT 1
230   VLIN 5,10 AT 19
240   PLOT 2,10
250   HLIN 3,4 AT 11
260   VLIN 11,12 AT 18
270   PLOT 17,13
280   HLIN 15,16 AT 14
290   PLOT 14,15: PLOT 13,16: PLOT
      4,16
300   VLIN 10,15 AT 5
310   HLIN 11,12 AT 17
320   PLOT 3,17: PLOT 2,18
330   PLOT 10,18: PLOT 9,19: PLOT
      8,20
340   PLOT 7,21
350   VLIN 19,20 AT 1
360   VLIN 21,23 AT 0
370   REM   DRAW BODY
380   HLIN 1,3 AT 24
390   HLIN 8,11 AT 22
400   PLOT 12,23: PLOT 14,26
410   VLIN 25,27 AT 4
420   VLIN 24,25 AT 13
430   HLIN 15,18 AT 27
440   HLIN 2,3 AT 28
450   VLIN 28,34 AT 2
460   VLIN 34,35 AT 3
470   HLIN 3,6 AT 31
480   PLOT 7,32: PLOT 8,33
```

```
490    HLIN 9,10 AT 34
500    VLIN 35,37 AT 11
510    VLIN 35,38 AT 12
520    VLIN 38,39 AT 13
530    PLOT 14,39
540    HLIN 13,17 AT 35
550    VLIN 35,36 AT 18
560    VLIN 34,37 AT 19
570    VLIN 36,37 AT 20
580    PLOT 21,37: PLOT 19,34
590    PLOT 20,33: PLOT 21,32
600    VLIN 29,31 AT 22
610    REM   DRAW HEAD
620    PLOT 19,26: PLOT 23,28
630    PLOT 24,27: PLOT 25,26
640    VLIN 22,25 AT 18
650    PLOT 17,21: PLOT 26,25
660    HLIN 19,20 AT 21
670    VLIN 23,24 AT 27
680    HLIN 21,24 AT 20
690    PLOT 25,21: PLOT 26,22
700    REM   DRAW EYE
710    PLOT 23,24
720    HLIN 23,24 AT 23
730    COLOR= 7
740    PLOT 24,24
750    REM   DRAW ACORN
760    COLOR= 8
770    HLIN 25,26 AT 34
780    HLIN 25,27 AT 35
790    HLIN 24,27 AT 36
800    HLIN 24,28 AT 37
810    HLIN 24,27 AT 38
820    COLOR= 13
830    PLOT 26,33: PLOT 28,38
840    VLIN 33,34 AT 27
850    VLIN 35,37 AT 29
860    VLIN 34,36 AT 28
870    END
```

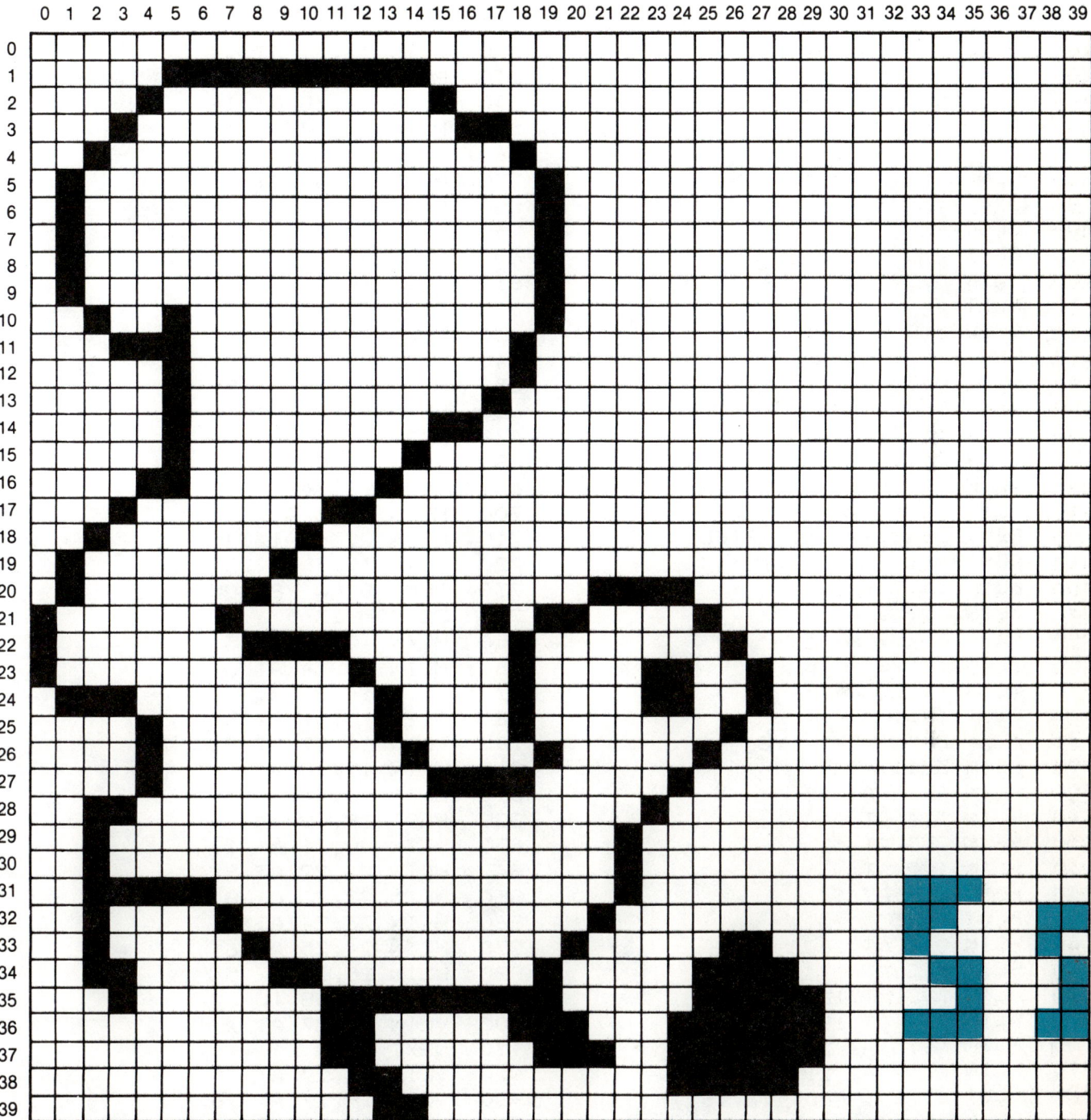

ALTERATIONS:

Add another acorn.
Add an oak leaf.
Make the squirrel gray.

totem

```
10    HOME
20    GR
30    REM   DRAW TOP OF TOTEM
40    COLOR= 8
50    FOR X = 0 TO 4
60    HLIN 0,39 AT X
70    NEXT X
80    COLOR= 2
90    FOR X = 5 TO 30
100   HLIN 0,39 AT X
110   NEXT X
120   COLOR= 8
130   FOR X = 0 TO 4
140   HLIN 0,39 AT X
150   NEXT X
160   HLIN 11,27 AT 32
170   VLIN 21,28 AT 15
180   VLIN 21,28 AT 23
190   HLIN 15,23 AT 28
200   REM   DRAW MAGENTA PIECES
210   COLOR= 1
220   HLIN 14,24 AT 5
230   HLIN 15,23 AT 6
240   HLIN 16,22 AT 7
250   HLIN 17,21 AT 8
260   HLIN 18,20 AT 9
270   PLOT 19,10
280   REM   DRAW LEFT EYE
290   HLIN 5,11 AT 9
300   HLIN 4,12 AT 10
310   HLIN 3,4 AT 11
320   HLIN 2,3 AT 12
330   HLIN 1,2 AT 13
340   HLIN 0,1 AT 14
350   PLOT 0,15
360   HLIN 0,1 AT 16
370   HLIN 1,2 AT 17
380   HLIN 2,3 AT 18
390   HLIN 3,4 AT 19
400   HLIN 4,15 AT 20
410   HLIN 5,11 AT 21
420   PLOT 15,19: PLOT 16,18
430   VLIN 15,17 AT 17
440   PLOT 16,14: PLOT 15,13
450   PLOT 14,12: PLOT 13,11
460   REM   DRAW RIGHT EYE
470   HLIN 27,33 AT 9
480   HLIN 26,34 AT 10
490   HLIN 34,35 AT 11
500   HLIN 35,36 AT 12
510   HLIN 36,37 AT 13
520   HLIN 37,38 AT 14
530   PLOT 38,15
540   HLIN 37,38 AT 16
550   HLIN 36,37 AT 17
560   HLIN 35,36 AT 18
570   HLIN 34,35 AT 19
580   HLIN 23,34 AT 20
590   HLIN 27,33 AT 21
600   PLOT 23,19: PLOT 22,18
610   VLIN 15,17 AT 21
620   PLOT 22,14: PLOT 23,13
630   PLOT 24,12: PLOT 25,11
640   REM   DRAW MOUTH
650   HLIN 14,24 AT 29
660   HLIN 12,26 AT 30
670   HLIN 8,30 AT 31
680   HLIN 4,10 AT 32
690   HLIN 28,34 AT 32
700   HLIN 3,35 AT 33
710   HLIN 2,36 AT 34
720   HLIN 1,37 AT 35
730   REM   DRAW YELLOW PIECES
740   COLOR= 13
750   HLIN 12,13 AT 5
760   HLIN 13,14 AT 6
770   HLIN 14,15 AT 7
780   HLIN 15,16 AT 8
790   HLIN 16,17 AT 9
800   HLIN 17,18 AT 10
810   HLIN 18,20 AT 11
820   PLOT 19,12
830   HLIN 20,21 AT 10
840   HLIN 21,22 AT 9
850   HLIN 22,23 AT 8
860   HLIN 23,24 AT 7
870   HLIN 24,25 AT 6
880   HLIN 25,26 AT 5
890   FOR X = 18 TO 20
900   VLIN 16,27 AT X
910   NEXT X
920   VLIN 18,27 AT 17
930   VLIN 19,27 AT 16
940   VLIN 18,27 AT 21
950   VLIN 19,27 AT 22
960   HLIN 6,14 AT 25
970   HLIN 5,14 AT 26
980   HLIN 4,14 AT 27
990   HLIN 3,14 AT 28
1000  HLIN 2,13 AT 29
1010  HLIN 1,11 AT 30
1020  HLIN 0,7 AT 31
```

```
1030    HLIN 0,3 AT 32
1040    HLIN 0,2 AT 33
1050    HLIN 0,1 AT 34
1060    PLOT 0,35
1070    FOR X = 36 TO 39
1080    HLIN 0,39 AT X
1090    NEXT X
1100    HLIN 24,32 AT 25
1110    HLIN 24,34 AT 26
1120    HLIN 24,35 AT 27
1130    HLIN 24,36 AT 28
1140    HLIN 25,37 AT 29
1150    HLIN 27,38 AT 30
1160    HLIN 31,39 AT 31
1170    HLIN 35,39 AT 32
1180    HLIN 36,39 AT 33
1190    HLIN 37,39 AT 34
1200    HLIN 38,39 AT 35
1210    COLOR= 0
1220    HLIN 5,12 AT 12
1230    HLIN 26,33 AT 12
1240    HLIN 4,13 AT 13
1250    HLIN 25,34 AT 13
1260    HLIN 4,10 AT 14
1270    HLIN 12,14 AT 14
1280    HLIN 24,26 AT 14
1290    HLIN 28,34 AT 14
1300    HLIN 4,10 AT 15
1310    HLIN 13,14 AT 15
1320    HLIN 24,26 AT 15
1330    HLIN 29,34 AT 15
1340    HLIN 4,14 AT 16
1350    HLIN 24,34 AT 16
1360    HLIN 4,14 AT 17
1370    HLIN 24,34 AT 17
1380    HLIN 5,14 AT 18
1390    HLIN 24,33 AT 18
1400    HLIN 5,13 AT 19
1410    HLIN 25,33 AT 19
1420    COLOR= 15
1430    PLOT 1,15: PLOT 37,15
1440    VLIN 14,16 AT 2
1450    VLIN 14,16 AT 36
1460    VLIN 13,17 AT 3
1470    VLIN 13,17 AT 35
1480    PLOT 4,12: PLOT 4,18
1490    PLOT 34,12: PLOT 34,18
1500    HLIN 5,12 AT 11
1510    HLIN 26,33 AT 11
1520    PLOT 13,12: PLOT 25,12
1530    HLIN 13,14 AT 13
1540    HLIN 24,25 AT 13
1550    VLIN 14,18 AT 15
1560    VLIN 14,18 AT 23
1570    VLIN 15,17 AT 16
1580    VLIN 15,17 AT 22
1590    PLOT 14,19: PLOT 24,19
1600    VLIN 14,15 AT 11
1610    VLIN 14,15 AT 27
1620    PLOT 12,15: PLOT 28,15
1630    REM   DRAW BIG T
1640    COLOR= 5
1650    HLIN 1,3 AT 1
1660    VLIN 1,6 AT 2
1670    REM   DRAW SMALL T
1680    VLIN 2,6 AT 5
1690    PLOT 4,3: PLOT 6,3
1700    END
```

ALTERATIONS:

Change the colors of the totem.

Make your own totem pole.

Make the totem's eyes blink red and white (just the centers).

UFO

```
10    HOME
20    GR
30    REM   DRAW LARGE U
40    COLOR= 13
50    VLIN 1,6 AT 10
60    VLIN 1,6 AT 12
70    PLOT 11,6
80    REM   DRAW SMALL U
90    VLIN 2,6 AT 15
100   VLIN 2,6 AT 17
110   PLOT 16,6
120   REM   DRAW TOP OF UFO
130   HLIN 14,20 AT 9
140   HLIN 21,22 AT 10
150   PLOT 23,11: PLOT 24,12
160   VLIN 13,14 AT 25
170   HLIN 25,26 AT 14
180   PLOT 24,15: PLOT 23,14: PLOT
      22,15
190   PLOT 21,14: PLOT 20,15: PLOT
      19,14
200   PLOT 18,15: PLOT 17,14: PLOT
      16,15
210   PLOT 15,14: PLOT 14,15: PLOT
      13,14
220   PLOT 12,15: PLOT 11,14: PLOT
      10,15
230   HLIN 8,9 AT 14
240   PLOT 9,13: PLOT 10,12: PLOT
      11,11
250   HLIN 12,13 AT 10
260   REM   DRAW BOTTOM OF UFO
270   HLIN 14,20 AT 26
280   PLOT 11,23: PLOT 23,23
290   PLOT 12,24: PLOT 22,24
300   PLOT 13,25: PLOT 21,25
310   REM   DRAW MIDDLE OF UFO
320   COLOR= 5
330   HLIN 3,31 AT 15
340   HLIN 3,31 AT 22
350   PLOT 2,16: PLOT 1,17: PLOT 0
      ,18
360   PLOT 1,19: PLOT 2,20: PLOT 3
      ,21
370   PLOT 32,16: PLOT 33,17
380   HLIN 33,34 AT 18
390   PLOT 33,19: PLOT 32,20: PLOT
      31,21
400   REM   DRAW DESIGN ON UFO
410   COLOR= 3
420   HLIN 2,32 AT 17
```

```
430    HLIN 2,32 AT 19
440    PLOT 3,18: PLOT 6,18: PLOT 9
       ,18
450    PLOT 12,18: PLOT 15,18: PLOT
       18,18
460    PLOT 21,18: PLOT 24,18: PLOT
       27,18
470    PLOT 30,18
480    REM   DRAW LETTERS-UFO
490    VLIN 30,35 AT 7
500    VLIN 30,35 AT 10
510    VLIN 30,35 AT 13
520    VLIN 30,35 AT 19
530    VLIN 30,35 AT 22
540    HLIN 8,9 AT 35
550    HLIN 14,16 AT 30
560    HLIN 14,15 AT 32
570    HLIN 20,21 AT 30
580    HLIN 20,21 AT 35
590    REM   DRAW SPACE THING
600    COLOR= 4
610    HLIN 26,34 AT 26
620    VLIN 27,35 AT 26
630    HLIN 26,34 AT 36
640    VLIN 27,35 AT 34
650    VLIN 37,39 AT 28
660    VLIN 37,39 AT 32
670    HLIN 26,27 AT 39
680    HLIN 33,34 AT 39
690    HLIN 24,25 AT 27
700    HLIN 35,36 AT 27
710    VLIN 28,30 AT 24
720    VLIN 28,30 AT 36
730    REM   DRAW FACE
740    COLOR= 11
750    PLOT 29,28: PLOT 31,28
760    PLOT 30,30
770    VLIN 31,32 AT 28
780    HLIN 29,31 AT 32
790    VLIN 32,33 AT 32
800    END
```

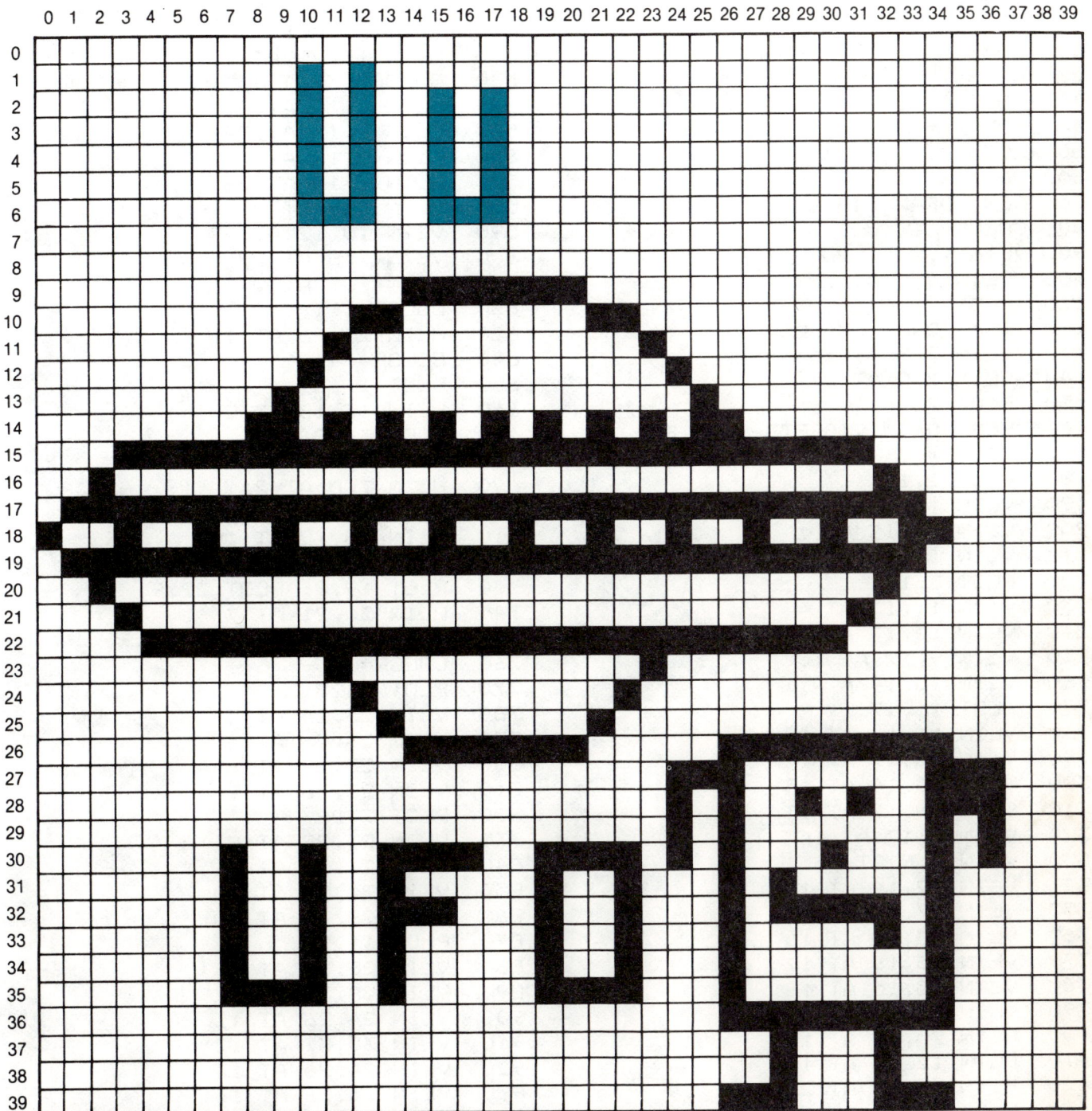

ALTERATIONS:

Make the visitor from space wave his arm.

Make the spaceship turn on its lights.

Add a small spaceman.

violets

```
10    HOME
20    GR
30    COLOR= 15
40    FOR X = 0 TO 39
50    HLIN 0,39 AT X
60    NEXT X
70    REM   DRAW BIG V
80    COLOR= 13
90    VLIN 1,5 AT 20
100   VLIN 1,5 AT 22
110   PLOT 21,6
120   REM   DRAW SMALL V
130   VLIN 2,5 AT 25
140   VLIN 2,5 AT 27
150   PLOT 26,6
160   REM   DRAW VIOLETS-PURPLE
170   COLOR= 3
180   PLOT 1,11
190   VLIN 14,15 AT 0
200   VLIN 13,15 AT 1
210   VLIN 12,14 AT 2
220   PLOT 3,13
230   VLIN 11,13 AT 4
240   VLIN 11,12 AT 5
250   VLIN 9,12 AT 10
260   VLIN 10,14 AT 11
270   PLOT 11,17
280   VLIN 11,14 AT 12
290   VLIN 16,17 AT 12
300   VLIN 13,14 AT 13
310   VLIN 16,17 AT 13
320   VLIN 9,17 AT 14
330   VLIN 8,9 AT 15
340   VLIN 12,14 AT 15
350   VLIN 17,19 AT 15
360   VLIN 13,20 AT 16
370   VLIN 15,16 AT 17
380   VLIN 15,15 AT 18
390   VLIN 16,22 AT 19
400   HLIN 20,22 AT 16
410   HLIN 12,13 AT 19
420   HLIN 11,12 AT 20
430   PLOT 12,21
440   COLOR= 11
450   PLOT 2,11
460   VLIN 11,12 AT 3
470   VLIN 10,11 AT 15
480   VLIN 9,12 AT 16
490   HLIN 11,12 AT 18
500   PLOT 11,19
510   HLIN 18,19 AT 14
520   HLIN 19,20 AT 15
530   COLOR= 3
540   VLIN 9,10 AT 23
550   VLIN 8,11 AT 24
560   VLIN 7,10 AT 25
570   VLIN 7,10 AT 26
580   VLIN 6,8 AT 27
590   VLIN 10,12 AT 27
600   VLIN 7,8 AT 28
610   VLIN 7,8 AT 29
620   COLOR= 11
630   HLIN 25,26 AT 11
640   COLOR= 4
650   PLOT 1,16
660   VLIN 15,18 AT 2
670   PLOT 3,19
680   HLIN 4,6 AT 20
690   HLIN 7,8 AT 21
700   PLOT 9,20
710   VLIN 18,19 AT 10
720   VLIN 9,13 AT 18
730   PLOT 19,8: PLOT 22,9
740   HLIN 20,21 AT 7
750   HLIN 21,23 AT 8
760   COLOR= 3
770   PLOT 4,23
780   VLIN 23,24 AT 5
790   VLIN 23,26 AT 6
800   VLIN 28,29 AT 6
810   VLIN 23,26 AT 7
820   PLOT 7,28
830   VLIN 23,29 AT 8
840   VLIN 21,26 AT 9
850   VLIN 21,26 AT 10
860   VLIN 28,30 AT 10
870   PLOT 11,23
880   VLIN 25,26 AT 11
890   VLIN 28,30 AT 11
900   VLIN 24,26 AT 12
910   VLIN 30,31 AT 12
920   VLIN 24,26 AT 13
930   VLIN 25,26 AT 14
940   COLOR= 13
950   HLIN 9,10 AT 27
960   COLOR= 11
970   HLIN 6,7 AT 27
980   PLOT 11,27
990   VLIN 28,29 AT 12
1000   COLOR= 3
1010   VLIN 18,22 AT 17
1020   VLIN 21,22 AT 18
```

```
1030  VLIN 25,26 AT 18
1040  VLIN 16,22 AT 19
1050  VLIN 18,29 AT 20
1060  VLIN 18,23 AT 21
1070  VLIN 25,26 AT 21
1080  VLIN 21,22 AT 22
1090  VLIN 26,27 AT 22
1100  VLIN 18,22 AT 23
1110  VLIN 26,27 AT 23
1120  VLIN 17,21 AT 24
1130  VLIN 26,28 AT 24
1140  VLIN 18,19 AT 25
1150  PLOT 25,27
1160  VLIN 23,23 AT 26
1170  VLIN 22,24 AT 27
1180  VLIN 16,19 AT 28
1190  VLIN 22,25 AT 28
1200  VLIN 15,23 AT 29
1210  VLIN 15,26 AT 30
1220  VLIN 19,22 AT 31
1230  PLOT 31,25
1240  VLIN 27,29 AT 31
1250  VLIN 18,25 AT 32
1260  VLIN 16,25 AT 33
1270  VLIN 16,20 AT 34
1280  VLIN 22,23 AT 34
1290  VLIN 25,26 AT 34
1300  VLIN 26,27 AT 35
1310  COLOR= 13
1320  VLIN 15,16 AT 15
1330  PLOT 21,24: PLOT 22,25
1340  VLIN 23,24 AT 31
1350  COLOR= 11
1360  HLIN 17,19 AT 23
1370  PLOT 18,24
1380  PLOT 22,24
1390  HLIN 23,24 AT 25
1400  HLIN 31,32 AT 26
1410  PLOT 32,27: PLOT 34,24
1420  VLIN 23,25 AT 35
1430  COLOR= 4
1440  VLIN 27,28 AT 14
1450  VLIN 29,30 AT 15
1460  VLIN 31,33 AT 16
1470  VLIN 25,30 AT 17
1480  VLIN 34,35 AT 17
1490  PLOT 18,36
1500  PLOT 21,29: PLOT 23,29
1510  VLIN 30,31 AT 22
1520  VLIN 25,26 AT 26
1530  PLOT 24,34: PLOT 11,34
1540  HLIN 8,9 AT 35
1550  VLIN 35,37 AT 12
1560  HLIN 10,13 AT 37
1570  VLIN 38,39 AT 14
1580  HLIN 1,5 AT 39
1590  HLIN 8,9 AT 38
1600  PLOT 10,39
1610  PLOT 23,32
1620  HLIN 21,23 AT 36
1630  VLIN 35,38 AT 25
1640  HLIN 24,29 AT 37
1650  PLOT 26,39
1660  COLOR= 12
1670  HLIN 10,13 AT 32
1680  HLIN 8,14 AT 33
1690  HLIN 7,10 AT 34
1700  HLIN 12,14 AT 34
1710  HLIN 6,7 AT 35
1720  HLIN 10,11 AT 35
1730  PLOT 13,35
1740  HLIN 6,11 AT 36
1750  HLIN 5,9 AT 37
1760  HLIN 14,15 AT 37
1770  HLIN 4,7 AT 38
1780  HLIN 10,13 AT 38
1790  HLIN 15,16 AT 38
1800  HLIN 6,9 AT 39
1810  HLIN 11,13 AT 39
1820  HLIN 15,16 AT 39
1830  VLIN 31,34 AT 25
1840  VLIN 32,34 AT 26
1850  HLIN 22,24 AT 33
1860  HLIN 21,23 AT 34
1870  HLIN 20,24 AT 35
1880  HLIN 19,20 AT 36
1890  VLIN 35,36 AT 24
1900  HLIN 18,23 AT 37
1910  HLIN 30,33 AT 37
1920  HLIN 18,24 AT 38
1930  HLIN 26,32 AT 38
1940  HLIN 18,25 AT 39
1950  HLIN 27,31 AT 39
1960  END
```

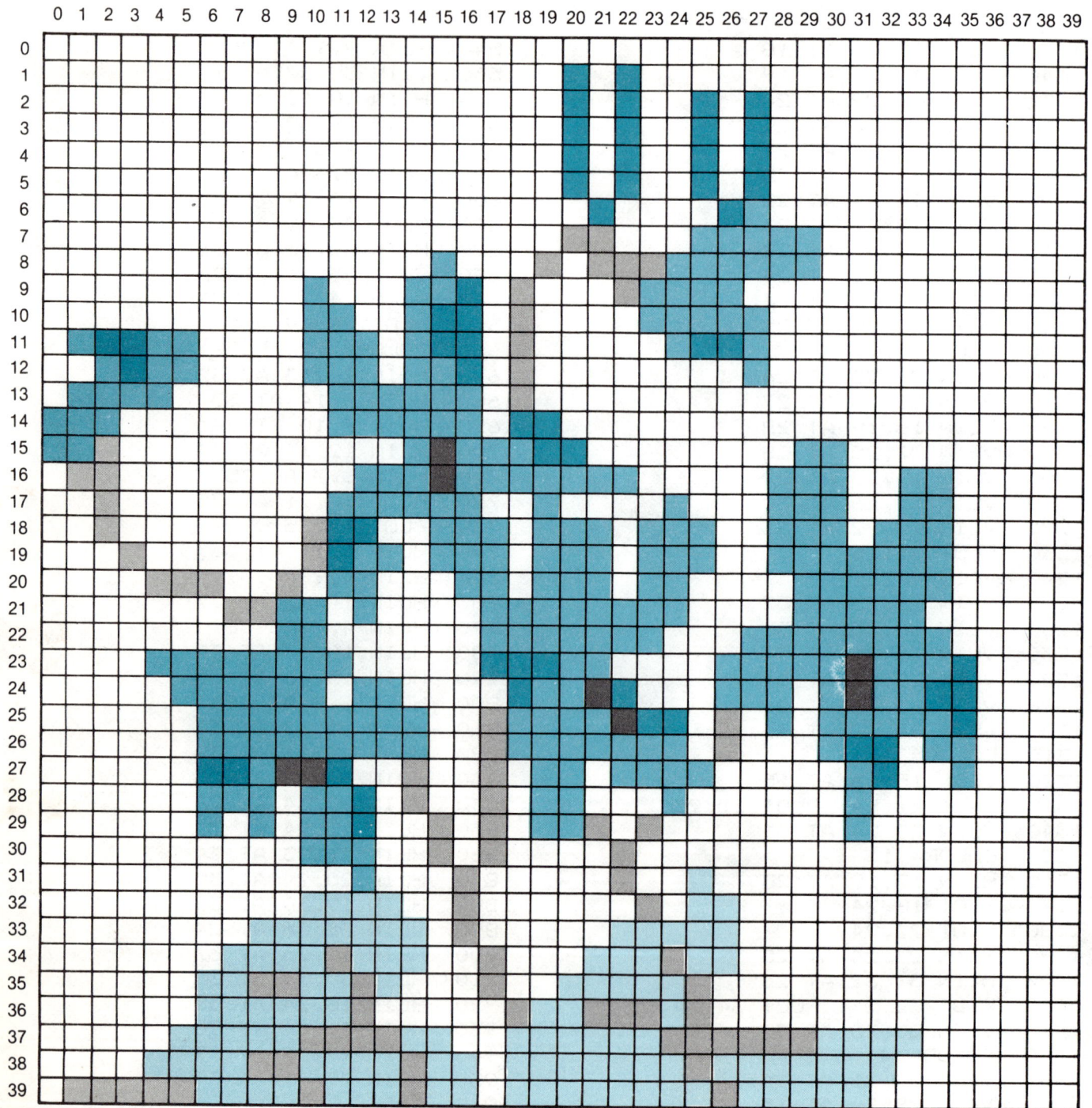

ALTERATIONS:
Add a honeybee.
Add a butterfly.
Add a dandelion.

watermelon slice

```
10   HOME
20   GR
30   REM   DRAW BIG W
40   COLOR= 4
50   VLIN 7,11 AT 1
60   VLIN 7,11 AT 3
70   VLIN 7,11 AT 5
80   PLOT 2,12: PLOT 4,12
90   REM   DRAW SMALL W
100   VLIN 8,11 AT 8
110   VLIN 8,11 AT 10
120   VLIN 8,11 AT 12
130   PLOT 9,12: PLOT 11,12
140   REM   DRAW RIND
150   COLOR= 12
160   HLIN 1,16 AT 32
170   HLIN 17,19 AT 31
180   HLIN 20,21 AT 30
190   HLIN 22,24 AT 29
200   PLOT 25,28: PLOT 26,27: PLOT
      27,26
210   VLIN 24,25 AT 28
220   PLOT 29,23
230   VLIN 20,22 AT 30
240   VLIN 3,19 AT 31
250   COLOR= 15
260   HLIN 2,16 AT 31
270   HLIN 16,19 AT 30
280   HLIN 20,21 AT 29
290   HLIN 21,24 AT 28
300   PLOT 25,27: PLOT 26,26: PLOT
      28,23
310   VLIN 24,25 AT 27
320   VLIN 20,22 AT 29
330   VLIN 5,19 AT 30
340   REM   DRAW MELON
350   COLOR= 1
360   HLIN 3,15 AT 30
370   HLIN 4,19 AT 29
380   HLIN 5,20 AT 28
390   HLIN 6,24 AT 27
400   HLIN 7,25 AT 26
410   HLIN 8,26 AT 25
420   HLIN 9,26 AT 24
430   HLIN 10,27 AT 23
440   HLIN 11,28 AT 22
450   HLIN 12,28 AT 21
460   HLIN 13,28 AT 20
470   HLIN 18,29 AT 19
480   HLIN 19,29 AT 18
490   HLIN 20,29 AT 17
```

```
500     HLIN 21,29 AT 16
510     HLIN 21,29 AT 15
520     HLIN 21,29 AT 14
530     HLIN 21,29 AT 13
540     HLIN 21,29 AT 12
550     HLIN 22,29 AT 11
560     HLIN 23,29 AT 10
570     HLIN 24,29 AT 9
580     HLIN 25,29 AT 8
590     HLIN 26,29 AT 7
600     HLIN 27,29 AT 6
610     HLIN 28,29 AT 5
620     HLIN 29,30 AT 4
630     PLOT 30,3
640     PRINT  TAB( 3)"WHO BIT MY ME
        LON?"
650     END
```

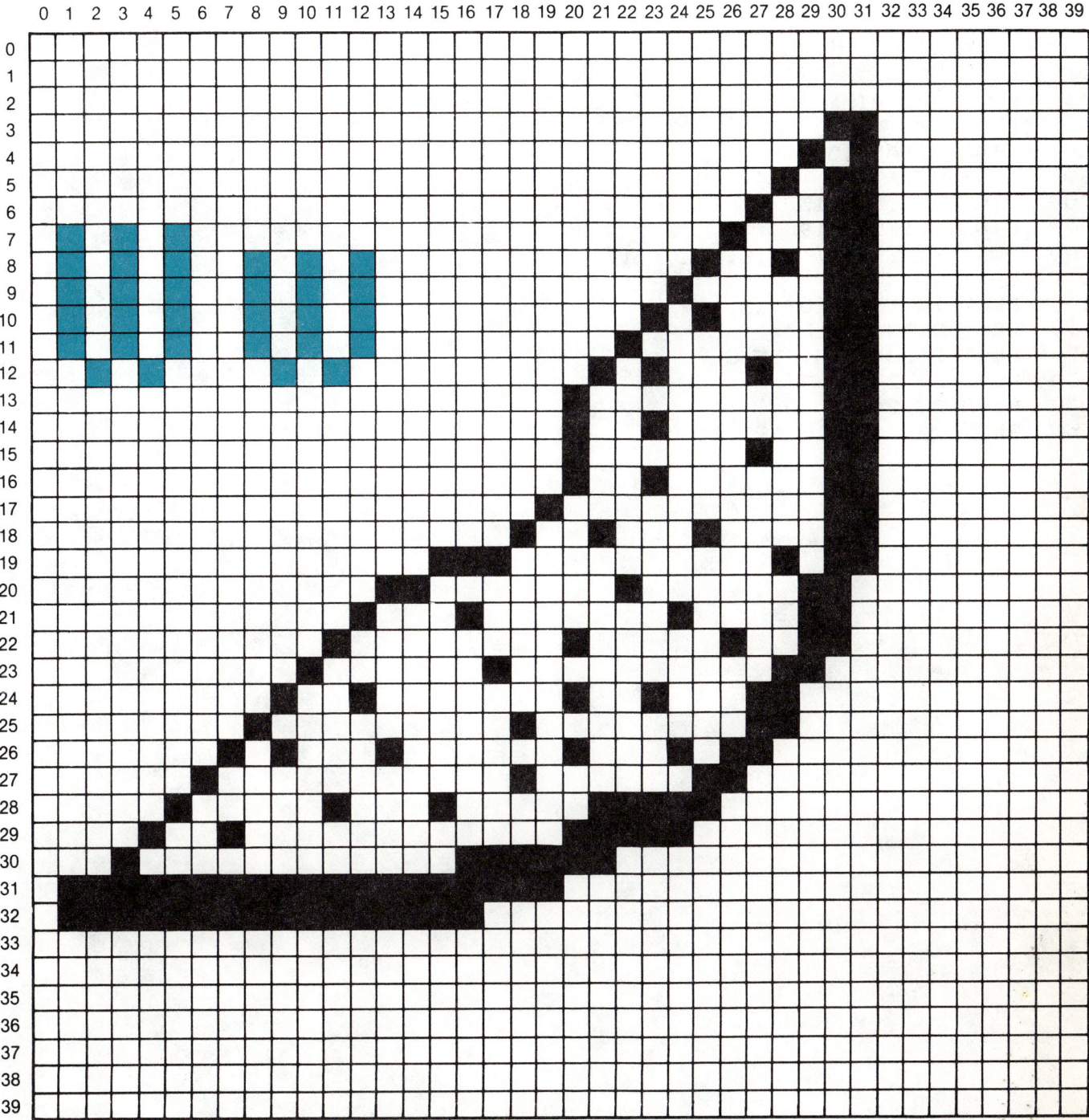

ALTERATIONS:

This diagram has seeds. The program on the diskette doesn't.
Add the seeds.
Add the words "Wonderful watery watermelon".

xanadu

```
10    HOME
20    GR
30    REM   DRAW BI X
40    COLOR= 9
50    VLIN 6,7 AT 15
60    VLIN 6,7 AT 19
70    VLIN 10,11 AT 15
80    VLIN 10,11 AT 19
90    PLOT 16,8: PLOT 18,8: PLOT 17
      ,9
100   PLOT 16,10: PLOT 18,10
110   REM   DRAW SMALL X
120   PLOT 22,8: PLOT 25,8
130   HLIN 23,24 AT 9
140   HLIN 23,24 AT 10
150   PLOT 22,11: PLOT 25,11
```

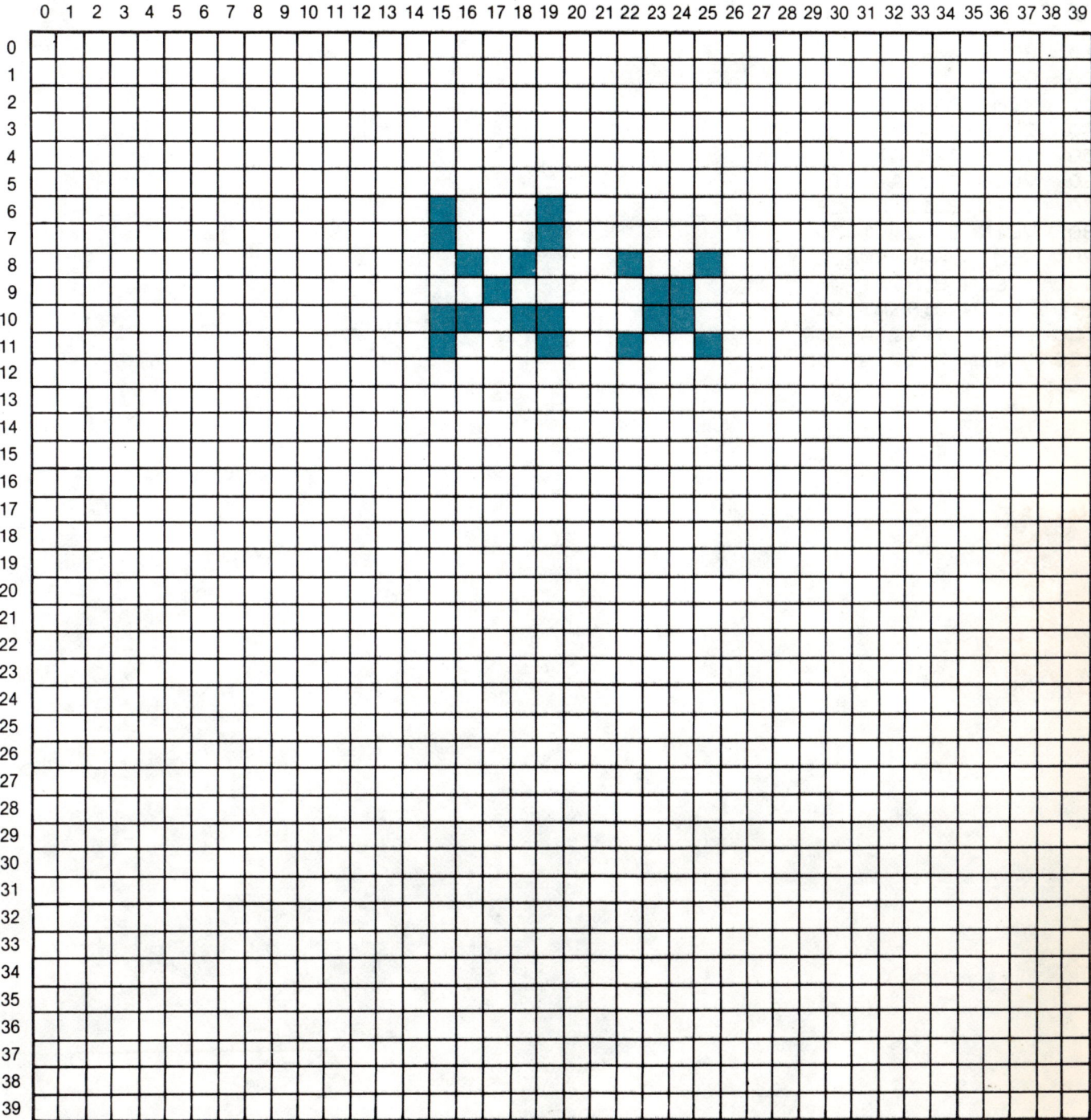

ALTERATIONS:
A great king once built a perfectly beautiful
palace.
He called it Xanadu.
Build your own palace. Will it have high
spires? A moat?

your favorite thing

```
10    HOME
20    GR
30    REM   DRAW BIG Y
40    COLOR= 13
50    VLIN 7,8 AT 28
60    VLIN 7,8 AT 31
70    VLIN 8,12 AT 29
80    VLIN 8,12 AT 30
90    REM   DRAW SMALL Y
100   VLIN 8,9 AT 33
110   VLIN 8,9 AT 36
120   VLIN 9,12 AT 34
130   VLIN 9,12 AT 35
```

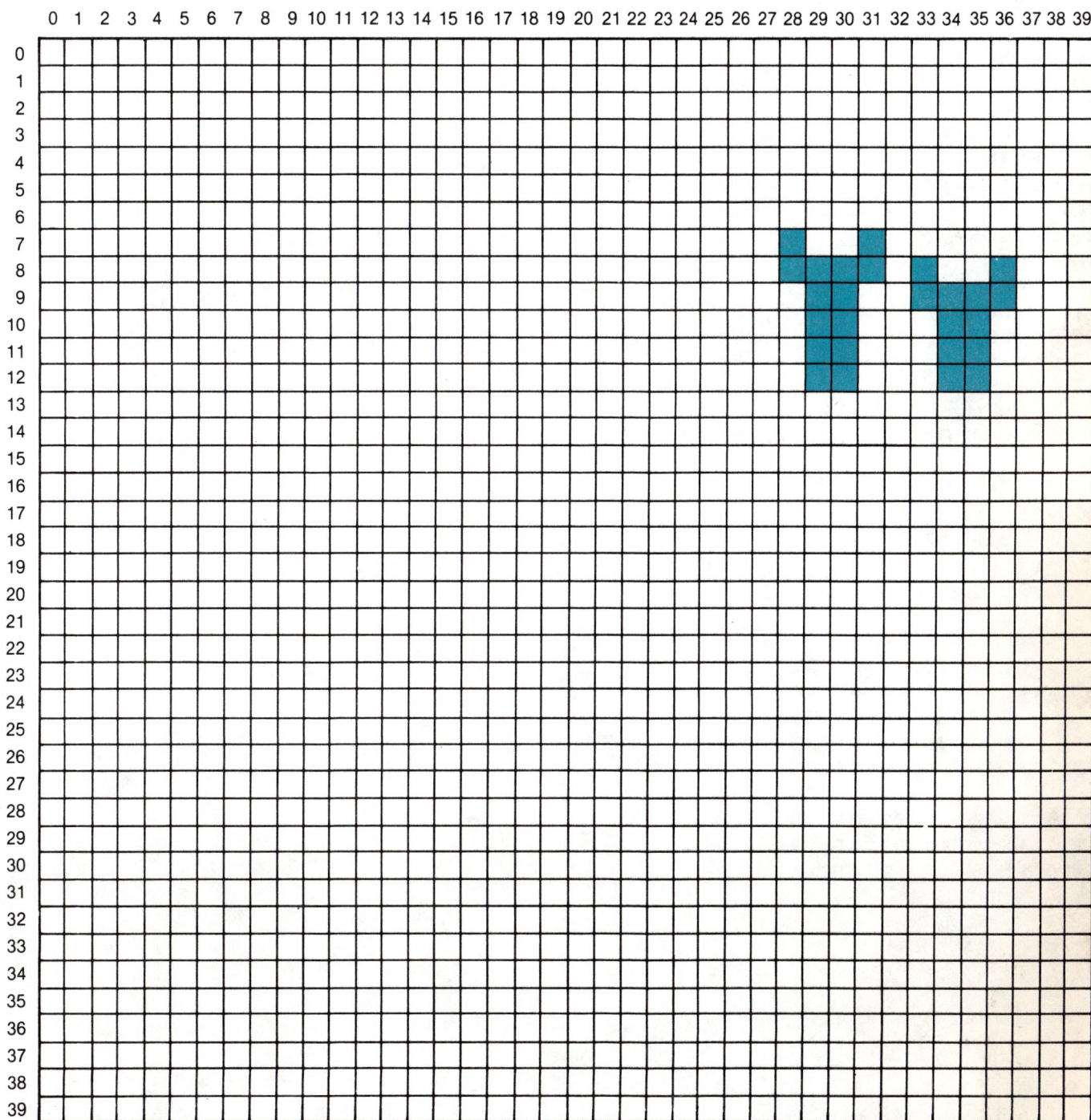

```
   0 1 2 3 4 5 6 7 8 9 10 11 12 13 14 15 16 17 18 19 20 21 22 23 24 25 26 27 28 29 30 31 32 33 34 35 36 37 38 39
 0
 1
 2
 3
 4
 5
 6
 7
 8
 9
10
11
12
13
...
39
```

ALTERATIONS:

Another blank worksheet—just for YOU!!
What is your favorite hobby, sport or book?
What is your favorite movie or television show?
Here's your chance to show the world what you
really love.

127

zipper

```
10   HOME
20   GR
30   COLOR= 4
40   FOR X = 39 TO 0 STEP  - 1
50   HLIN 11,23 AT X
60   NEXT X
70   REM   DRAW BIG Z
80   COLOR= 7
90   HLIN 0,3 AT 16
100   HLIN 0,3 AT 21
110   PLOT 3,17: PLOT 2,18
120   PLOT 1,19: PLOT 0,20
130   REM   DRAW SMALL Z
140   HLIN 6,9 AT 17
150   HLIN 6,9 AT 21
160   PLOT 8,18: PLOT 7,19: PLOT 6
      ,20
170   REM   DRAW ZIPPER
180   COLOR= 5
190   VLIN 12,39 AT 17
200   PLOT 16,11: PLOT 18,11
210   PLOT 15,10: PLOT 19,10
220   VLIN 2,9 AT 14
230   VLIN 2,9 AT 20
240   HLIN 15,19 AT 37
250   HLIN 15,19 AT 34
260   HLIN 15,19 AT 31
270   HLIN 15,19 AT 28
280   HLIN 15,19 AT 25
290   HLIN 15,19 AT 22
300   VLIN 13,22 AT 15
310   VLIN 13,22 AT 19
320   HLIN 15,19 AT 13
330   END
```

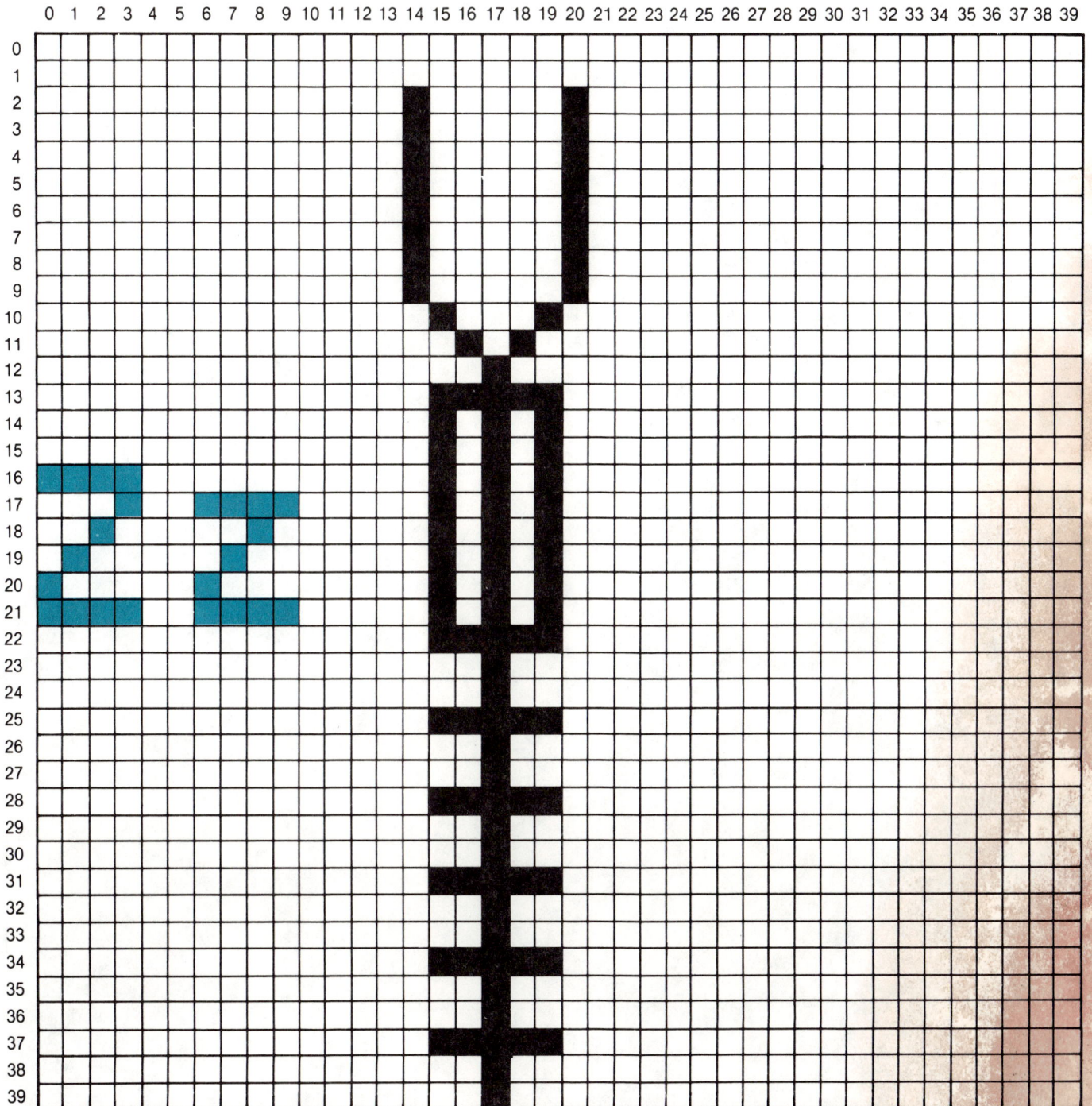

ALTERATIONS:

Add the word zipper.

Add other z words.

Now keep on working on new ideas.

Further fantasies
7

Many people have a fantasy of letting the computer do boring or silly jobs. We are going to make this fantasy true for you.

This chapter is called "Further Fantasies" because it shows you how to make the computer work better for you. If you have had some practice from Chapters 5 and 6, you will be able to make your pictures faster!

Let's start now.

Type the following short program:

```
10   HOME
20   GR
30   COLOR= 15
40   FOR X = 0 TO 39
50   VLIN 0,39 AT X
60   NEXT X
```

Type RUN

There you have a completely white screen, fast and simple.

X is a variable. That means its value changes. X is not equal to only one number. It can be equal to many numbers.

By using line 4Ø, you told the computer to draw a VLIN from Ø to 39 AT every value of X. The computer drew the VLIN from Ø to 39 AT Ø
1
2
3
4

and the rest of the numbers to 39.

Then it stopped because it ran out of numbers.

You can control how far the computer draws lines, because you tell it what numbers X stands for.

X could be equal to Ø to 5, or 18 to 24, or 14 to 39. Whenever you want a solid block of lines, you can use X.

Let's experiment!!

Add these lines to your program:

```
70   COLOR= 12
80   VLIN 0,39 AT 19
90   HLIN 0,39 AT 19
```

Type RUN

We now have four white boxes.

Let's change the upper left box to magenta.

```
100   COLOR= 1
110   FOR X = ___ TO ___
```
The block of magenta will start at row _____ and end at row _____.

```
120   HLIN ___,___ AT X
```
Command to draw line at all values stated for X

```
130   NEXT X
```
You will have an error message if you do not have a NEXT statement.

```
140   COLOR= 5
```
Now change the upper right box to gray.

```
150   FOR X = ___ TO ___
```
The block of gray will start at row _____ and end at row _____.

```
160   HLIN ___,___ AT X
```
Command to draw line at all values stated for X.

```
170   NEXT X
```
Don't forget NEXT!!!!

```
180   COLOR= 9
190   FOR X = ___ TO ___
```
Block of orange will start at row _____ and end at row _____.
(Bottom left)

```
200   HLIN ___,___ AT X
210   NEXT X
220   COLOR= 14
230   FOR X = ___ TO ___
240   HLIN ___,___ AT X
250   NEXT X
```

Do the last block by
yourself.
(Bottom right)

REMEMBER:
VLINS AND HLINS
NEED A BEGINNING,
END, AND ROW OR
COLUMN TO DESCRIBE
WHERE THEY ARE.
X IS FOLLOWED BY
AN EQUAL TO SIGN(=)
AND STATES THE
NUMBER TO BEGIN
AND END WITH.

FOUR COLOR BLOCKS, SIMPLE AND BEAUTIFUL AND SUPER FAST.

Instead of 18 commands to draw 1 block of color, you used only 4. You saved typing 14 lines.

Practice with FOR X= different values.

Don't forget NEXT.

Here are the answers to the block commands on page 133 and above.

```
110   FOR X = 0 TO 18
120   HLIN 0,18 AT X
150   FOR X = 0 TO 18
160   HLIN 20,39 AT X
190   FOR X = 20 TO 39
200   HLIN 0,18 AT X
230   FOR X = 20 TO 39
240   HLIN 20,39 AT X
```

BACKGROUNDS

Now that you can control many VLINs and HLINs at the same time, you can make a background for the pictures in Chapters 5 and 6.

To add backgrounds, we simply change the program lines in the beginning of the program.

The background must be drawn first. The rest of the picture is drawn over the background.

Let's look at the boat program.

```
10    HOME
20    GR
30    COLOR= 2
40    REM   DRAW BIG B
ETC.
```

As Chapter 1 said, we used line numbers 10,20,30, etc., just in case we forgot a command. We didn't forget, but we do have room for changing several commands. We can also add numbers in between.

Run the B program so it is in the computer's memory.

Type TEXT

Type LIST 10,40

Are you ready to change the B program?

Let's go!

Type the following commands.

```
2    HOME
4    GR
6    COLOR= 5                sets color to gray.
7    REM   DRAW SKY          sets value for top and
8    FOR X = 0 TO 12         bottom of sky.
10   HLIN 0,39 AT X          draws sky HLINs.
12   NEXT X                  tells computer to keep
                             going.
                             until it runs out of
                             numbers.

14   COLOR= 14               sets color to aqua.
15   REM   DRAW SEA
16   FOR X = 13 TO 39        sets value for top and
                             bottom of sea.
18   HLIN 0,39 AT X          draws sea HLINs.
20   NEXT X                  tells the computer to keep
                             going until it runs out of
                             numbers.
```

Type RUN

MAGIC!! A new program!

You can choose different colors. You may also want to add a rock or a lighthouse using FOR-NEXT statements.

If you want to keep these changes, you must SAVE the boat program. Type SAVE and the name you want it SAVEd under. Press the return and it's done.

Go on to Chapters 5 and 6. Make some backgrounds.

Then come back to Chapter 7 for something really NEAT!!

BACKGROUNDS II

We can also make color bars for our backgrounds. We can use the FOR-NEXT statements with the STEP variation. The statement STEP will tell the computer how to use the values stated for X.

Type the following: (Don't forget NEW!)

```
10   GR
20   COLOR= 15
30   FOR X = 0 TO 39 STEP 2
40   VLIN 0,39 AT X
50   NEXT X
```

Type RUN and you have bars of color!!

The computer uses the first number ($\emptyset$), then adds 2 to get the next number. The second number is 2. It adds 2 again to get the third number which is 4. It continues until it reaches the end of the numbers (39).

Change line 4$\emptyset$ to

```
40   HLIN 0,39 AT X
```

What happens? The bars run the other way.

STEP LETS US JUMP OVER NUMBERS WE DON'T WANT TO USE.

I LOVE STEP 6 AND 8

Change the number that follows STEP. Use 4,5,6, etc., to see the different bar patterns you can make. Remember to write down the STEP statement for the ones you like. You can use them for backgrounds.

We can experiment with the STEP statement in another way.

Type the following:

```
30  FOR X = 39 TO 0 STEP - 2
```
THE minus sign is next to the reset key

In this line, the computer starts with 39 and subtracts the STEP number to make the numbers that show where the VLINs will be.

Experiment with bars and blocks of color. Draw the lines from right to left and left to right. Draw them from the top to the bottom and from the bottom to the top.

For more fun, get a worksheet and:

THINK about a color block design.

PLAN what colors will be used and how the blocks and bars will appear on the screen.

WRITE the commands on a WRITE COMMANDS Worksheet.

DO the program.

This is the letter Q activity. You can design your own CRAZY QUILT.

Now that you know how to use HLINs and VLINs with X, you are probably wondering about PLOT.

We can use a variable with PLOT, but we will use two. We'll also use the STEP command.

Type and RUN this program:

```
10    HOME
20    GR
30    COLOR= 15
40    FOR X = 0 TO 39 STEP 2
50    VLIN 0,39 AT X
60    HLIN 0,39 AT X

70    NEXT X
```

Both VLIN and HLIN will use the same values for X.

That's quite a checkerboard, isn't it?

Now, how would you like to fill in all those cute little empty spaces?????

Impossible, you say?

How could you doubt Mr. Graphix?

Type the following lines and RUN the program.

```
80    COLOR= 12
90    FOR X = 30 TO 0 STEP  - 2
100   FOR Y = 39 TO 0 STEP  - 2
110   PLOT X,Y
120   NEXT Y
130   NEXT X
```

NEXT Y comes before X
NEXT X must be last
Y must be "nested" in X.
Just remember before and your programs will be fine.

Type RUN

See smartie!!

How do you like that!

I'll expect my apology in the mail by next Friday, at the latest.

This program works like others that use X to hold a value for certain numbers.

In this case, X= the numbers 39,37,35,33, etc.

STEP-2 subtracts 2 to get the next number.

This time we have also added another variable called Y, because PLOT needs two numbers. The values for X and Y will be the same.

But the computer did the work, not us. We didn't get tired fingers from PLOTting all the green boxes with separate commands. Look at the typing time we saved!!!

That was fun!

Here are more ways to have fun with variables and PLOT.

Type them all and see what they do.Write neatly by the ones you like best. You may want to use them later in one of your own programs. They are a present to you from me!!!!

PINK DOTS

```
10   HOME
20   GR
30   COLOR= 11
40   FOR X = 0 TO 39 STEP 2
50   FOR Y = 0 TO 39 STEP 6
60   PLOT X,Y
70   NEXT Y
80   NEXT X
```

BLUE DOTS

```
10   HOME
20   GR
30   COLOR= 7
40   FOR X = 0 TO 39 STEP 4
50   FOR Y = 0 TO 39 STEP 4
60   PLOT X,Y
70   NEXT Y
80   NEXT X
```

GREEN DOTS

```
10   HOME
20   GR
30   COLOR= 12
40   FOR X = 0 TO 39 STEP 5
50   FOR Y = 0 TO 39 STEP 5
60   PLOT X,Y
70   NEXT Y
80   NEXT X
```

SHEETING BLUE

```
10   HOME
20   GR
30   COLOR= 2
40   FOR X = 0 TO 39
50   FOR Y = 0 TO 39
60   PLOT X,Y
70   NEXT Y
80   NEXT X
```

Here are my favorite two!! Put them with sheeting blue and it is BEAUTIFUL!!!!

GRAY LINES

```
10    HOME
20    GR
30    COLOR= 10
40    FOR X = 39 TO 0 STEP  - 1
50    FOR Y = 39 TO 0 STEP  - 2
60    PLOT X,Y
70    NEXT Y
80    NEXT X
```

REVERSE SHEETING BLUE

```
10    HOME
20    GR
30    COLOR= 2
40    FOR X = 39 TO 0 STEP  - 1
50    FOR Y = 39 TO 0 STEP  - 1
60    PLOT X,Y
70    NEXT Y
80    NEXT X
```

MY FAVORITE BORDER

```
10    HOME
20    GR
30    COLOR= 15
40    FOR X = 0 TO 39
50    HLIN 0,39 AT X
60    NEXT X
70    COLOR= 0
80    FOR X - 0 TO 39 STEP 4
90    VLIN 39,36 AT X
100   HLIN 39,36 AT X
110   VLIN 0,4 AT X
120   HLIN 0,4 AT X
130   NEXT X
```

SOUND

You can make your programs fancier by using attention-grabbing sounds. A simple way is to use the CTRL key and the G key. By using the quotation mark and the CTRL-G(Bell), you can add sound in a second!

Type this short program to see how sound is made:

```
10    GR
20    COLOR= 9
30    FOR X = 0 TO 19
40    PRINT " "
50    HLIN 0,19 AT X
60    NEXT X
```

Type the word PRINT followed by a quotation mark. Hold down the CTRL key and type the G(bell) key at the same time. Make another quotation mark.
You may use the SHIFT? as a short form for PRINT.

NOISY COLOR!! By adding sound, you make your program even snappier.

Since the sound made by the CTRL-G may be high for some ears, we can make lower sounds. But, as usual, we need commands.

SOUND tells the computer it will be making sounds

PEEK tells the computer to look at a certain part of its memory.

This formula for sound is very hard to explain. So we won't bother. We'll just learn to use it as it is.

Type the following:

```
10   GR
20   FOR C = 1 TO 15        Sets a variable for making
                            colors change.
30   COLOR= C               COLOR command is
                            turned into the variable C.
40   FOR X = 0 TO 39        Shows where the HLIN's
                            lines will be drawn.
50   HLIN 0,29 AT X         DRAWS the lines.
60 S =  - 16336             Save typing time in next
                            statement.
70 SOUND =  PEEK (S)        Creates a click.
80   NEXT X                 Tells computer to draw
                            next HLIN.
90   NEXT C                 Tells computer to use next
                            color.
```

Type RUN and enjoy the soft click as the screen changes colors.

Experiment with SOUND by adding and subtracting the PEEK(S) part of line 7Ø

EXAMPLE:

7Ø SOUND=PEEK(S)+PEEK(S)+PEEK(S)−PEEK(S)

Enjoy Sound. Both ways are fun and exciting.

Go to Chapters 5 and 6 and finish all your programs.

When you are sure you are done, read Chapter 8.

In Chapter 8, we will learn how to create a slide show of all our programs. As usual it will be fast, fun, and exciting!!

HAVE FUN!! SEE YOU SOON!!!

Computer slide shows
8

Well, you sure are a long way from the time when you didn't know a GR from a PLOT.

I'm proud of you. I'm sure you are proud of your work, too.

You can PLOT, VLIN, and HLIN. You even make X and Y do some of the work for you. You are a genius.

I'll bet you like to show off your programs.

How would you like to make a show of all your programs?

We can tie them together so they RUN one after the other.

Sounds great doesn't it?

You will need to learn a few commands, but that hasn't bothered you yet.

Let's begin.

In order to tie our programs together, we will need some very special commands.

These commands will tell the computer to RUN programs on the diskette where you have been saving them.

You will need to change the beginning and the ending lines of the programs you want in your slide show.

Let's use programs A and B for our examples.

First, type LOAD A or whatever you named the apple program.

In this case, LOAD A tells the computer to place A in its memory.

Type LIST 10,30

You should have something that looks like the following. If it doesn't exactly, it's okay. We will add the important line.

LOAD tells the computer to place a specific program in its memory.

BEGINNING

```
10   HOME
20   GR
30   REM   DRAW LARGE A
```

WE NEED TO MAKE THESE CHANGES:

```
5 D$ =   CHR$ (4)
```

If you have added a background to program A and B, just make sure the D$ command is the first line in your program.

That takes care of the beginning changes.

Now we must take care of the end commands.

Here's what the end will look like.

Type LIST and you will see the last commands of program A.

ENDING

```
410   PLOT 8,13: PLOT 9,12: PLOT 1
      0,11
420   END
```

The new ending should look like this:

```
414   FOR PAUSE = 1 TO 1000:
      NEXT PAUSE
```

Here's a new command. PAUSE tells the computer to wait before it goes to the next command. You can make the PAUSE as long as you want by making the number after the "to" larger. Don't add commas to numbers over 1000.

PAUSE tells the computer to wait before it goes on the next command.

We need the PAUSE to SLOW DOWN the computer. If we don't use PAUSE, the screens change too fast. LINES 415–418 add a screen wipe. More about them later.

```
415   COLOR= 15
416   FOR X = 0 TO 39
417   VLIN 0,39 AT X
418   NEXT X
420   PRINT D$" RUN B"
```

This command tells the computer to RUN the B program after it finishes A.

```
430   END
```

PAUSE tells the computer to wait before it goes to the next command.

Now comes the most *important* step!!!!

SAVE the A program so all your hard work is not lost!

Type SAVE A or whatever you have named the program.

You can save it under A1 or A2 if you want to keep your original program.

A is now finished. Let's work on B.

Type LOAD B and press the return.

LIST 1Ø,3Ø

BEGINNING:

```
10   HOME
20   GR
30   COLOR= 2
```

CHANGE B TO LOOK LIKE THIS:

```
 5 D$ =  CHR$ (4)
10   HOME
20   GR
30   COLOR= 2
```

If you are ready to tie another program to B, then you will change the last lines of B. Tell the computer which program you want to run next. It can be C,H,L,S, or U. It can be whatever program you would like it to be.

When you are finished—Type SAVE B.

Type RUN A and B will follow automatically.

I talked about "screen wipe" earlier.

The purpose of a screen wipe is to "dress up" your slide show. It is nice and fancy. It clears the first graphic picture from the screen.

We add screen wipes to the end of a program, just before the command to RUN the next program.

We can use VLINs, HLINs, or PLOTtings as screen wipes.

Check Chapter 7 for Sheeting and Reverse Sheeting.

This is one of my favorite screen wipes.

I call it the GREEN V. Type it and run it, and see why!!

```
10   COLOR= 12
20   FOR X = 0 TO 39
30   HLIN 0,39 AT X
40   VLIN 0,39 AT X
50   NEXT X
```

This will be at the end, but it does make a nice background, too.

Graphic slide shows are fun, but remember to go slow, put the commands in the right place, and SAVE the changed program back to the diskette.

Have fun creating your own slide shows. I'm proud of you. Now is the time for you to show off all you've learned!!

In review

Place the letter of the definition in front of the word it describes.

_____ ? SYNTAX ERROR

_____ FOR-NEXT

_____ STEP

_____ SOUND

_____ CTRL-G

_____ BELL

_____ LOAD A

_____ PAUSE

_____ SCREEN WIPE

_____ PRINT D$" RUN BOAT"

_____ PEEK

a. tells the computer to LOAD program A into its memory.
b. a message printed to the screen when the computer does not understand what has been typed.
c. tells the computer to wait before doing its next command.
d. word written on G key for sound.
e. a pattern which erases a graphic picture before the next one is drawn.
f. tells the computer to get ready to make sound.
g. tells the computer to look at a part of its memory.
h. simple way to make sound-bell ringing.
i. tells computer how to use values for X in FOR-NEXT statements.
j. tells computer values for certain commands and to keep going until all numbers are used.
k. tells the computer to RUN the boat program stored on the diskette.

GRAPHIX GRADE BOX

CORRECT

8–10

5–7

0–4

Photographic
graphics
9

A challenge for you!!

Design the perfect gift for everyone you love.

What can you do with your graphic abilities?

Take a look at the world around you.

Take apart the most familiar things. What do you see?

Triangles, rectangles, squares, dots, steps?

Triangles in triangles, rectangles on top of and next to rectangles—designs and patterns surround us.

Take what you see and give it to someone. That is a true gift, something from yourself, from your mind to another's.

THINK of a design.

PLAN it on paper.

WRITE the commands.

DO the program.

Then photograph it.

Ask your teacher or a parent if you can use their 35 mm camera. Maybe your school has a camera club or a media specialist who is a camera bug.

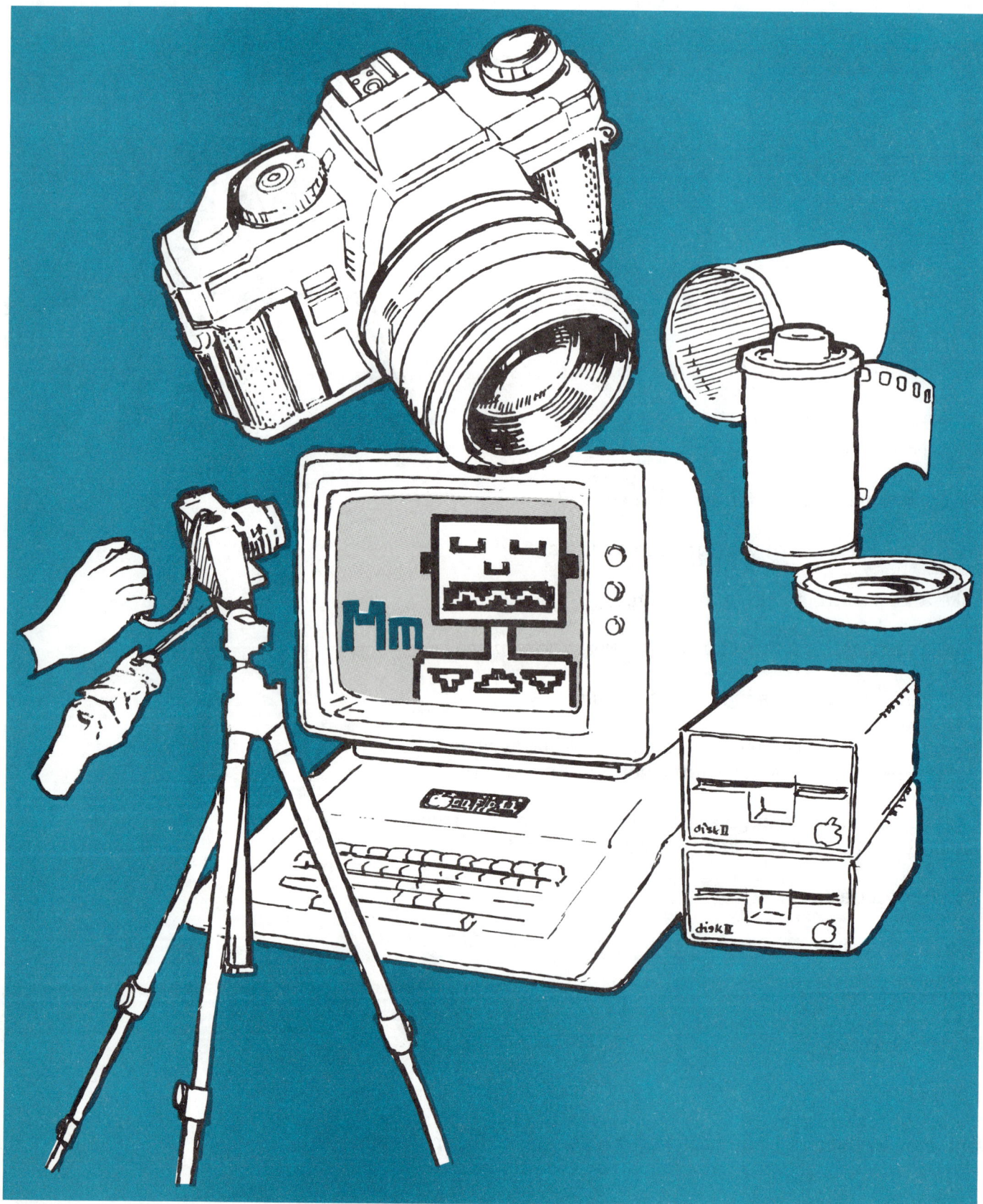

With your program and their camera, you can create the perfect photographic graphic gift.

Give your graphics as birthday presents or gifts for all occasions.

You will need several things to complete this project:

a program
a 35 mm camera
a cable release for the camera
steady hands or a tripod
and FILM!!

Arrange a quiet time with you and your program and your photographer.

RUN your program and turn the tint and color knobs until your program looks the way you want it to.

Turn up the brightness so that the colors in your program are very bright, but not blurry or distorted.

Focus the camera on the screen.

What do you see??

Do you see any glare?

What reflections do you see in the screen?

For the perfect picture, you will need to eliminate these distractions.

Shield your screen with cardboard, so there's no glare.

Turn off specific room lights that cause a glare.

Move your camera to an angle where it can't be seen.

Films with an ASA rating of 64 or 100 will give you the best pictures. The ASA rating tells how fast the film reacts to light. Make sure your ASA rating knob on the camera is set correctly.

Set camera shutter speed to 1/60th of a second. Use your light indicator. You may need to set it down to 1/4th of a second to get enough light to the film.

That is why you have a shutter release cable. If you have a

tripod, it would be a good idea to use that. This will prevent the camera from being jarred. Any movement will cause a blur.

Take several shots at different settings, from 1/8th to 1/2.

If all goes well, your pictures will be beautiful.

When your pictures return from the store, your personalized gifts are ready for giving.

You may want to create a special Christmas scene and photograph it. This picture can then be made into Christmas photo cards. Many stores run specials on this type of card in November. Take advantage of the bargain and amaze your relatives who live far away.

The best gift is one that comes from the heart, except maybe one that comes from our imagination.

Chapter 10 is for you, too.

It's all about high-resolution graphics—drawing with specks of light, not boxes of light.

SEE YOU THERE!!!!

HI-RES ready
10

Now that you are a pro at low-resolution graphics, how about a hi-res lesson?

High-resolution graphics uses tiny dots and thin lines of light to draw graphics.

Let's type and talk as we go along.

Use your diskette to turn on the computer.

Type HGR
Do I remind you to press the return?

NO!!

You're a PRO!!

The screen is totally black. Where's the cursor?

Type TEXT

Type HGR and the cursor appears, this time.

Now we're ready.

In high-resolution graphics we have eight colors to work with.

Ø	black1	4	black2
1	green	5	orange
2	violet	6	blue
3	white1	7	white2

Type HCOLOR=3

To plot points in hi-res, we need two numbers as we did in low-res. The only difference is the size of the plot and the size of the screen.

In hi-res, the vertical counters are Ø to 279.

The horizontal counters are Ø to 159.

Type HPLOT 1ØØ,1ØØ

HPLOT tells the computer to turn on a light 1ØØ to the right and 1ØØ down.

We have a tiny white dot.

Type HPLOT 179,1ØØ

We now have two tiny white dots.

This could take us forever to draw if we draw dot by dot.

Let's learn how to make lines with the HPLOT command.

Making lines in hi-res is fun and easy.

We need to tell the computer a beginning point and an end point. The computer does the rest.

The two points on the screen will be our beginning and ending points.

The word TO is the important word. It tells the computer to draw from one point TO another point.

Type HPLOT 1ØØ,1ØØ TO 179,1ØØ

Nice line!

Type HPLOT Ø,Ø TO 279,Ø

Can you guess where this line will appear before you press the return?

A horizontal line across the top of the screen.

Type HPLOT Ø,159 TO 279,159

That's the bottom horizontal line.

If the screen is Ø to 279 across the top and Ø to 159 along the side, what is the command to draw a vertical line along the left side of the screen?

What is the command to draw a vertical line along the right side of the screen?

Your answers should be:

LEFT SIDE HPLOT Ø,Ø TO Ø,159

RIGHT SIDE HPLOT 279,Ø TO 279,159

Here's another activity to practice on.

Connect the upper left corner with the lower right corner.

Connect the lower left corner with the upper right corner.

Even diagonal lines are easy with hi-res.

FIRST DIAGONAL HPLOT Ø,Ø TO 279,159

SECOND DIAGONAL HPLOT Ø,159 TO 279,Ø

FAST AND EASY!!

Now that you understand the HPLOT command, let's take a closer look at our screen for hi-res.

Type the following program.

```
10   HGR
20   HCOLOR= 3
30   HPLOT 0,0 TO 279,0
40   HPLOT 279,0 TO 279,159
50   HPLOT 279,159 TO 0,159
60   HPLOT 0,159 TO 0,0
70   REM  DRAW VERTICAL CENTER
80   HPLOT 140,0 TO 140,159
90   REM  DRAW HORIZONTAL CENTER
100   HPLOT 0,80 TO 279,80
```

Lines 30–60 draw a rectangle.

Type RUN.

We now have four rectangles.

Each rectangle is 140 units across the top and 80 units along the side. We can use these rectangles to guide our drawings.

```
Ø,Ø                        140,Ø                      279,Ø
┌─────────────────────────────┬─────────────────────────────┐
│                             │                             │
│          7Ø,4Ø              │          21Ø,4Ø             │
│                             │                             │
Ø,79 ─────────────────────────┼───────────────────────────── 279,79
│                             │                             │
│          7Ø,12Ø             │          21Ø,12Ø            │
│                             │                             │
└─────────────────────────────┴─────────────────────────────┘
Ø,159                      14Ø,159                   279,159
```

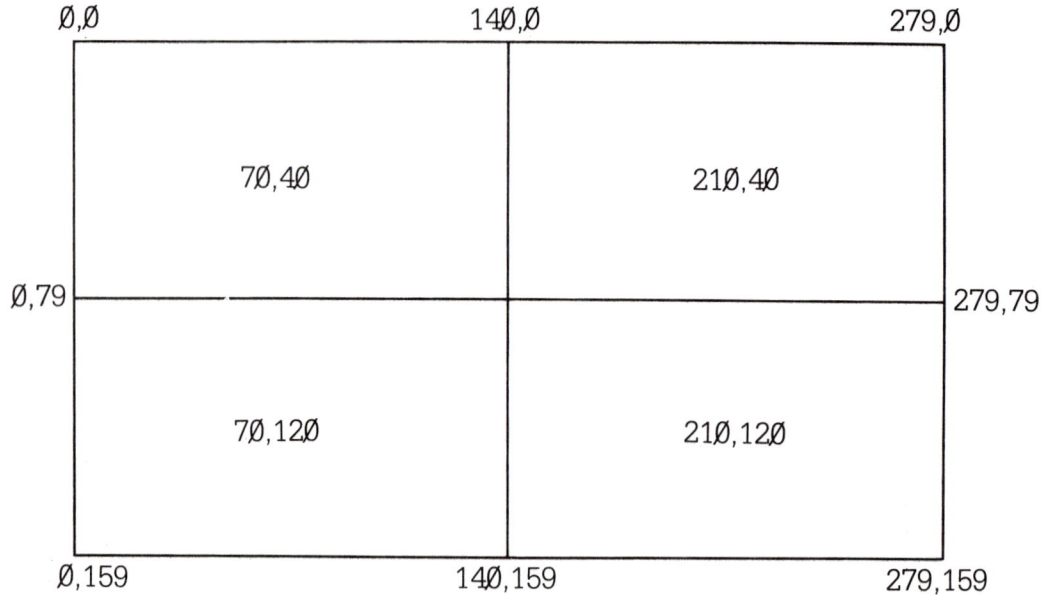

Let's plot four more points. We'll plot the centers of the four rectangles.

```
110    REM   DRAW CENTERS
120    HPLOT 70,40
130    HPLOT 210,40
140    HPLOT 70,120
150    HPLOT 210,120
```

These numbers will help us find the points we need to draw lines.

Type RUN

Type TEXT

Type LIST

Now we can connect these four dots. We can do it in one command. Are you ready for an exciting part of hi-res?

Type the following lines.

```
155 REM DRAW CENTER RECTANGLE
160 HPLOT 70,40 TO 210,40 TO
    210,120 TO 70,120 TO
    70,40
```

HPLOT can be used to draw from one point to another in a series of lines. Pick four points and HPLOT them together line by line.

Type RUN.

Now that's fast drawing!!

Our program now draws:

> an outer frame
> a vertical center
> a horizontal center
> and an inner rectangle.

These points, as listed on the diagram on page 5, will help you plot your drawings.

But first, we must SAVE this program.

Type S VE SK BS   SK BS will mean Sketch
                                                Base.

And I even have a plan for you to use when drawing in hi-res.

The plan is simple. Although it has five parts, each part is easy.

1. ADD   We'll add commands to SK BS to draw our letters.
2. DEL   We'll delete the extra commands.
3. RUN   We'll run the new program
4. SAVE   We'll save the new program
5. LOAD   We'll LOAD SK BS and start over again with a
                    new idea.

Let's start with the letter A.

Without typing TEXT, type LIST, so we can see the last command we typed.

There it is—

```
160 HPLOT 70,40 TO 210,40 TO
    210,120 TO 70,120 TO
    70,40
```

Type these lines to ADD A:

```
165 REM DRAW A
170 HCOLOR = 1
180 HPLOT 105,120 TO 105,20
    TO 175,20 TO 175,120
190 HPLOT 105,70 TO 175,70
200 END
```
                                       That's green.

                                       Your A is finished.

Type DEL 20,160   This removes the sketch
                                            lines that guide your
                                              drawing.

Type RUN	Now you can see what A looks like.
Type SAVE A	This puts your A program on your diskette.
Type LOAD SK BS	This loads the sketch base program. You are now ready to start your next letter.

X is an easy letter to draw.

Now that SK BS is in memory, type LIST ADD the following lines:

```
165   DRAW X
170   HCOLOR= 6
180   HPLOT 70,40 TO 210,120
190   HPLOT 70,120 TO 210,40
200   END
```

170 — That's blue.
180/190 — An easy way to draw X is to connect the opposite corners of the inner rectangle.

Type DEL 20,160	Good-bye to the sketch base.
Type RUN	Isn't that a nice X?
Type SAVE X	X is now on your diskette

That's pretty easy isn't it?

The fun had just begun. Try creating letters of the alphabet for practice. When you feel comfortable with hi-res, come back to Adding Variables. There we will add the variables we learned to use in Chapter 7.

ADDING VARIABLES

In Chapter 7, we stated a range of numbers for the computer to use while drawing many VLINs and HLINs. We can use that FOR-NEXT command setup in hi-res, too.

To draw boxes and other shapes, X will be a very handy thing to have.

Type these short programs and explore the world of hi-res
graphics.

BLUE RECTANGLE

```
10    HGR
20    HCOLOR= 6
30    FOR X = 0 TO 5
40    FOR Y = 0 TO 80
50    HPLOT 0,0 TO X,Y
60    NEXT Y
70    NEXT X
80    END
```

PURPLE PINCERS

```
10    HGR
20    HCOLOR= 2
30    FOR X = 100 TO 110
40    FOR Y = 90 TO 100
50    HPLOT 0,0 TO X,Y
60    NEXT Y
70    NEXT X
80    END
```

ORANGE FLARE

```
10    HGR
20    HCOLOR= 5
30    FOR X = 250 TO 279
40    FOR Y = 129 TO 149
50    HPLOT 279,159 TO X,Y
60    HPLOT 279,0 TO X,Y
70    NEXT Y
80    NEXT X
90    END
```

GREEN BOX

```
10    HGR
20    HCOLOR= 1
30    FOR X = 130 TO 150
40    FOR Y = 70 TO 90
50    HPLOT 140,80 TO X,Y
60    NEXT Y
70    NEXT X
80    END
```

BLUE FLASH

```
10    HGR
20    HCOLOR= 6
30    FOR X = 270 TO 279
40    FOR Y = 0 TO 9
50    HPLOT 75,100TOX,Y
60    NEXT Y
70    NEXT X
80    END
```

GREEN FLASH

```
10    HGR
20    HCOLOR= 1
30    FOR X = 180 TO 200
40    FOR Y = 139 TO 159
50    HPLOT 140,80 TO X,Y
60    NEXT Y
70    NEXT X
80    END
```

PURPLE PYRAMID

```
10    HGR
20    HCOLOR= 2
30    FOR X = 70 TO 130
40    HPLOT 100,0 TO X,159
50    NEXT X
60    END
```

ORANGE PYRAMID

```
10    HGR
20    HCOLOR= 5
30    FOR X = 120 TO 160
40    HPLOT 140,80 TO X,159
50    NEXT X
60    END
```

BLUE PYRAMID

```
10   HGR
20   HCOLOR= 6
30   FOR X = 110 TO 150
40   HPLOT 130,159 TO X,Y
50   NEXT X
60   END
```

BLUE BLOCK

```
10   HGR
20   HCOLOR= 6
30   FOR X = 0 TO 10
40   FOR Y = 0 TO 10
50   HPLOT 0,0 TO X,Y
60   NEXT Y
70   NEXT X
80   END
```

CHAPTER 10 SUPPLEMENT

In addition to making designs with variables, we can use them in a different way with HGR to make solid shapes. The formula for a solid background is simple, if we look at what the program says.

Type NEW and the following program. We will add to it as we go along.

```
10    HGR
20    HCOLOR= 3
30    REM  FOR A SOLID BACKGROUND
40    FOR N = 0 TO 159
50    HPLOT 0,0 + N TO 279,0 + N
60    NEXT N
```

Type RUN

In this part of the program, we tell the computer to HPLOT a line from Ø,Ø to 279,Ø and add the value of N from Ø to 159. In this way, each line of the background is HPLOTted a line at a time from the top(Ø) to the bottom(159).

Every value of N from Ø to 159 is used:

```
HPLOT 0,0 +0 TO 279,0 +0
HPLOT 0,0 +1 TO 279,0 +1
HPLOT 0,0 +2 TO 279,0 +2
```

. . . . ALL THE WAY TO . . . .

```
HPLOT 0,0 + 159 TO 279,0 +159
```

We can use this same idea to make solid rectangles.

Type : LIST and type the next part of the program.

```
70    REM  FOR A SMALL RECTANGLE
80    HCOLOR= 5
90    FOR N = 0 TO 25
100   HPLOT 0,0 + N TO 15,0 + N
110   NEXT N
```

Type RUN

Again, the numbers for N move the lines down one at a time.

We don't need to start our rectangles at Ø,Ø. We can start any

place on the screen. We need to be careful though. Our values for N when added to X or Y must not go over 279 for X and 159 for Y.

If our numbers are larger than they should be, we will receive an error message (ILLEGAL QUANTITY ERROR).

Let's make a large rectangle this time and place it lower on the screen.

```
120   REM  FOR A BIG RECTANGLE
130   HCOLOR= 1
140   FOR N = 1 TO 50
150   HPLOT 50,50 + N TO 100,50 +
      N
160   NEXT N
```

Before we reach the special treat at the end of our DEMO program, we need a short lesson. We'll SAVE DEMO and finish it later.

Type SAVE DEMO

Type NEW and read on.

Here is a short lesson on the three new commands used at the end of the DEMO program.

GOTO: The GOTO command tells the computer to leave the normal program execution and GOTO a specific line number we type. We will use it to demonstrate the commands RANDOM and INT.

RND (1) will generate random numbers between Ø and 1.

Type and try this short program to see some very strange numbers.

```
10 X =  RND (1)
20   PRINT X
30   GOTO 10
```
There's a GOTO.

Type RUN

```
10 X =  RND (1)        ]RUN
20   PRINT X           .843382097
30   GOTO 10           .765147483
                       .0339702095
                       .746274339
```

```
.637794049
.0164948049
.216243014
.663247324
.724415478
.282472581
.561767149
.834610331
.15737394
.227399402
.0151581551
.475982707
.310782771
.388043993
.237029406
.331495742
.21233445
```

Watch the numbers for a while, then use CTRL C to stop the program. Remember to hold down the CTRL key, then type C.

Since RANDOM numbers are generated as decimals, we need to multiply them by a number to create a whole number. We will use the number 6, because we want numbers from Ø–5. For numbers Ø–3 we would multiply by 4.

REMEMBER:

We always multiply by 1 larger than the highest number we want because Ø is included in the range of numbers. RND (1) * 6 gives us numbers based on 0,1,2,3,4,5—SIX NUMBERS

Retype line number 1Ø to look like this:

```
10 X =  RND (1) * 6
```

Now type RUN.

You will see a display similar to this one. Your display won't match mine since the numbers are RANDOM.

```
10 X =  RND (1) * 6        ]RUN
20   PRINT X               1.26452557
30   GOTO 10               .581521724
                           2.47378083
                           .292313069
                           2.77261611
                           3.43425918
                           .433746747
                           1.77338677
                           5.77277142
```

```
5.98599912
4.26198067
3.13499433
3.24431696
3.82100943
3.79394385
5.98217722
3.907712
```

You will also need to use CTRL C to stop this program.

We still need to get rid of those decimals and the decimal point. We can do that easily with the INT command.

INT is short for integer. The purpose of INT is to make whole numbers out of numbers with decimals. It simply chops off the decimal. It does not round off numbers.

Retype line 10 so it looks like this:

```
10 X=INT(RND(1) * 6))
```

This line does three things.
1. Generates a random number
2. Multiplies it by 6
3. Drops the decimal point and all numbers after it.

Type RUN and you will see random whole numbers like the ones below.

```
10 X = INT ( RND (1) * 6)     ]RUN
20    PRINT X                   4
30    GOTO 10                   5
                               5
                               1
                               4
                               2
                               1
                               2
                               0
                               4
                               4
                               2
                               5
                               3
                               1
                               4
                               2
                               5
                               5
```

```
                          3
                          1
                          4
                          0
```

They won't come in the same order, because they are RANDOM.
Use CTRL C to stop this program also.

Now after all that, we can LOAD DEMO and finish typing the
last exciting commands.

```
170 HCOLOR=5
180 REM FOR A RECTANGLE THAT
    CHANGES COLORS AT RANDOM
190 X=120 :Y=20
200 FOR N=0 TO 100
210 HPLOT X,Y TO X+N,Y TO
    X+N,Y+N TO X,Y+N TO X,Y
220 HCOLOR=INT(RND (1) * 6)
230 NEXT N
240 GOTO 190
```

**REMEMBER (:) LET'S
PUT MORE THAN ONE
COMMAND ON A LINE.**

Type RUN. Use CTRL C to stop this program.

Instead of ending at line 240, the DEMO program goes to line
190. It follows through to line 240. At line 240, it is told to GOTO
190. This way, this program will never stop because it goes from
240 to 190 again and again. It is in an endless loop in RANDOM
color.

Here is the complete listing for DEMO:

```
10   HGR
20   HCOLOR= 3
30   REM  FOR A SOLID BACKGROUND
40   FOR N = 0 TO 159
50   HPLOT 0,0 + N TO 279,0 + N
60   NEXT N
70   REM  FOR A SMALL RECTANGLE
80   HCOLOR= 5
90   FOR N = 0 TO 25
100  HPLOT 0,0 + N TO 15,0 + N
110  NEXT N
120  REM  FOR A BIG RECTANGLE
130  HCOLOR= 1
140  FOR N = 1 TO 50
150  HPLOT 50,50 + N TO 100,50 +
     N
160  NEXT N
170  HCOLOR= 5
```

```
180   REM  FOR A RECTANGLE THAT CH
      ANGES COLORS AT RANDOM
190 X = 120:Y = 20
200   FOR N = 0 TO 100
210   HPLOT X,Y TO X + N,Y TO X +
      N,Y + N TO X,Y + N TO X,Y
220   HCOLOR=  INT ( RND (1) * 6)
230   NEXT N
240   GOTO 190
```

Experiment by placing rectangles at different places on the screen.

Can you make a triangle or a pentagon that changes color? You should be able to now. Plot the points on paper and use a range of numbers with N.

REMEMBER: LINE BY LINE!

Now that you know about GOTO, GOTO Unit J and make the pumpkin's eyes blink and make the light in Unit L: Lamp flash.

There are many uses for GOTO and you will find them in almost any program you design.

The world of Apple Graphics is a very large world. You have taken just a few small steps, but you have taken them well. Your imagination and creativity will take you even further. Almost anything you want to do will be done by plenty of :

THINKING
PLANNING
WRITING
AND . . . . . DOING!

SO GET GOING! Maybe I'll see you soon, in another book.

In review

_____ HGR

_____ TEXT

_____ HPLOT

_____ LOW-RESOLUTION GRAPHICS

_____ HIGH-RESOLUTION GRAPHICS

_____ HPLOT 1ØØ,125

_____ HPLOT 125,1ØØ TO Ø,Ø

_____ HCOLOR =

_____ HCOLOR=6

_____ HCOLOR=5

a. command to plot a dot of light on the screen.
b. command to use color in hi-res.
c. command to plot a dot 1ØØ over and 125 down.
d. command to turn on the hi-res screen.
e. drawing with specks and thin lines of light.
f. drawing with rectangles or boxes of light.
g. command to turn off graphics.
h. command to plot a line from point 125,1ØØ to point Ø,Ø.
i. command to use the color blue in hi-res.
j. command to use the color orange in hi-res.

GRAPHIX GRADE BOX

CORRECT

8–10

5–7

0–4

Appendix A
Teacher management system sheets

PRACTICE REVIEWS

Student or teacher can keep this form in a folder to keep a record of the scores on the practice review.

PLAN WORKSHEET

This worksheet allows the student to plan his work before the writing of commands.

Teachers may also use this form to give students an informal test. The teacher draws a certain figure on the worksheet. Then the students write the commands to draw the figure. The teacher may also add his own alterations at the bottom of the worksheet.

PROGRAM LOG SHEET

This form is for the student. He can keep a record of the programs completed, date they were completed, and the name the program was saved under. This form may be kept in a folder in the student's desk, or the teacher may place each log sheet in a folder for each class.

WRITE COMMANDS WORKSHEET

This worksheet allows the students an easy method of preplanning programming time. The worksheet may be filled out in class or at home before the student works on the computer.

PRACTICE REVIEWS

	STUDENT NAME	
	# POSSIBLE	SCORE
Practice Review 1	**12**	_____
Practice Review 2	**10**	_____
Practice Review 3	**8**	_____
Practice Review 4, 7, 8	**10**	_____
Practice Review 10	**10**	_____

PLAN WORKSHEET

	0	1	2	3	4	5	6	7	8	9	10	11	12	13	14	15	16	17	18	19	20	21	22	23	24	25	26	27	28	29	30	31	32	33	34	35	36	37	38	39
0																																								
1																																								
2																																								
3																																								
4																																								
5																																								
6																																								
7																																								
8																																								
9																																								
10																																								
11																																								
12																																								
13																																								
14																																								
15																																								
16																																								
17																																								
18																																								
19																																								
20																																								
21																																								
22																																								
23																																								
24																																								
25																																								
26																																								
27																																								
28																																								
29																																								
30																																								
31																																								
32																																								
33																																								
34																																								
35																																								
36																																								
37																																								
38																																								
39																																								

ALTERATIONS:

PROGRAM LOG SHEET

_____

STUDENT NAME

PROGRAM	DATE	SAVED UNDER THIS NAME
A	____ . .	_____
B	____ . .	_____
C	____ . .	_____
D	____ . .	_____
E	____ . .	_____
F	____ . .	_____
G	____ . .	_____
H	____ . .	_____
I	____ . .	_____
J	____ . .	_____
K	____ . .	_____
L	____ . .	_____
M	____ . .	_____
N	____ . .	_____
O	____ . .	_____
P	____ . .	_____
Q	____ . .	_____
R	____ . .	_____
S	____ . .	_____
T	____ . .	_____
U	____ . .	_____

V . . . . ———— .. ————————————————————

W . . . . ———— .. ————————————————————

X . . . . ———— .. ————————————————————

Y . . . . ———— .. ————————————————————

Z . . . . ———— .. ————————————————————

WRITE COMMANDS WORKSHEET

110 _____	1260 _____	1510 _____
120 _____	1270 _____	1520 _____
130 _____	1280 _____	1530 _____
140 _____	1290 _____	1540 _____
150 _____	1300 _____	1550 _____
160 _____	1310 _____	1560 _____
170 _____	1320 _____	1570 _____
180 _____	1330 _____	1580 _____
190 _____	1340 _____	1590 _____
1100 _____	1350 _____	1600 _____
1110 _____	1360 _____	1610 _____
1120 _____	1370 _____	1620 _____
1130 _____	1380 _____	1630 _____
1140 _____	1390 _____	1640 _____
1150 _____	1400 _____	1650 _____
1160 _____	1410 _____	1660 _____
1170 _____	1420 _____	1670 _____
1180 _____	1430 _____	1680 _____
1190 _____	1440 _____	1690 _____
1200 _____	1450 _____	1700 _____
1210 _____	1460 _____	1710 _____
1220 _____	1470 _____	1720 _____
1230 _____	1480 _____	1730 _____
1240 _____	1490 _____	1740 _____
1250 _____	1500 _____	1750 _____

Appendix B
Answers to "in reviews"

ANSWERS TO "IN REVIEW" CHAPTER 1

__K__ PROGRAMMING

__H__ APPLESOFT BASIC

__D__ COMMANDS

__J__ PROGRAM

__I__ LINE NUMBER

__C__ CURSOR

__B__ NEW

__E__ HOME

__L__ INIT

__G__ PRINT

__F__ LIST

__A__ RUN

ANSWERS TO "IN REVIEW" CHAPTER 2

__C__ GR

__E__ COLOR=

__B__ PLOT _____,_____

__F__ VERTICAL COLUMNS

__D__ HORIZONTAL ROWS

__G__ THINK

__H__ PLAN

__I__ WRITE

__J__ DO

__A__ SMILE

ANSWERS TO "IN REVIEW" CHAPTER 3

__D__ VLIN _____,_____ AT __

__F__ HLIN _____,_____ AT __

__C__ HOME

__B__ REM

__A__ TEXT

__E__ LIST

__G__ SAVE

__H__ LIST 20,60

ANSWERS TO "IN REVIEW" CHAPTER 8

__B__ ? SYNTAX ERROR

__J__ FOR NEXT

__I__ STEP

__F__ SOUND

__H__ CTRL-G

__D__ BELL

__A__ LOAD A

___C___ PAUSE

___E___ SCREEN WIPE

___K___ PRINT D$"RUN BOAT"

___G___ PEEK

ANSWERS TO "IN REVIEW" FOR CHAPTER 10

___D___ HGR

___G___ TEXT

___A___ HPLOT

___F___ LOW-RESOLUTION GRAPHICS

___E___ HIGH-RESOLUTION GRAPHICS

___C___ HPLOT 100,125

___H___ HPLOT 125,100 to 0,0

___B___ HCOLOR=

___I___ HCOLOR=6

___J___ HCOLOR=5

Appendix C
Teacher hints

How To Use This Book

The first four chapters should be used as small group or demonstration lessons. This will provide students with an initial exposure to the flow of procedures needed for programming in low resolution graphics.

After you work through this book, you will see other possibilities yourself. The last page of this book is just the beginning for you. The exciting part of programming is one idea leads to another and another and another . . .

The activities in the practice units of Chapter 5 & 6 were designed to be created by students in one thirty to forty-five minute period. The enhancements are sure to take as long as the students wish.

Some information in Chapter 7 will need teacher reinforcement, but your brighter students will be able to do it independently.

Don't rush to finish. Let the students explore, discover, create and DO.

The programming adventure is just beginning!

Projects for graphics are everywhere. Once your students can do graphics, they can start writing programs to help others learn. This will take practice, but they will want that practice. The following ideas incorporate the use of graphics.

PICTURE POEMS

When students write poems for language arts class, have them create graphic pictures with the text printed on the text lines of the graphics screen. A pause may be inserted between each line printed for ease of reading.

GRAPHIC SPEECHES

When students give a speech, they can prepare visuals to add detail to their speech.

Students can illustrate many topics from science, mathematics, and social studies. Art concepts lend themselves well to graphic interpretation.

SCIENCE	MATHEMATICS	SOCIAL STUDIES
food chains	geometric figures	charts on population
water cycle	number operations	role of president
flower parts	Venn diagrams	time lines

Give the children one idea and they will get thousands of inspirations.

GRAPHIC GAMES

Graphic games are like those in the supplement to Chapter 4.

Games can be used to teach programming skills. They can be enjoyed after several weeks of diligent work.

Glossary

Applesoft BASIC A programming language used by Apple computers. It is a variation of Microsoft BASIC used in microcomputers.

CATALOG A command which tells the computer to print out a list of all the programs on the diskette.

Colon(:) A colon can be used to put more than one command on a single line number. Example—9Ø PLOT 1Ø,15:PLOT13,15:PLOT 18,15.

COLOR= Command which tells the computer what color you want to draw with. There are 16 colors available in low-resolution graphics on the Apple II Plus computer.

Commands Commands are words in a programming language that tell the computer what to do.

CTRL-C This command will break into a running program. It will stop a program so commands can be added.

CTRL-G Sound can be made using the control key and the G key. To make a beep, type PRINT " "- between the quotation marks, hold down the control key and press the G(bell) key.

CTRL-S This command will stop a program or listing. Commands cannot be added using a CTRl-S.

Cursor The cursor is a flashing box of light on the monitor's screen. It shows the location of the next letter or number to be typed.

D$=CHR$(4) Special command for tying programs together for a graphics screen slide show.

END This command tells the computer it has reached the end of the program.

FOR-NEXT These two commands tell the computer to do the commands in between them FOR a certain number of times. example—FOR X=Ø to 5 NEXT X, FOR X=18 to 24 NEXT X, etc.

GR This command tells the computer you want to draw low-resolution graphics. It leaves four lines at the bottom of the screen to see what is being typed. COLOR= command must follow GR in order to see what is drawn on the screen.

HLIN _____,_____ **AT** _____ This command tells the computer to draw a horizontal line from one point to another at a certain row.

HOME This command tells the computer to clear the text from the screen and place the cursor at the upper left corner.

Horizontal Counters Horizontal counters number the horizontal rows. They are also used to measure the length of vertical lines.

Illegal Quantity Error Syntax error when you try to PLOT a number more than 39. This may also occur with VLINs or HLINs. See SYNTAX ERROR for more.

INIT This command tells the computer to initialize a diskette. Diskettes must be initialized before they can store programs. Programs used to initialize a diskette RUN automatically when the computer is turned on.

Line Numbers Every command in a program must have a line number. The computer does commands starting from the lowest line number.

LIST This command tells the computer to print commands of a program to the screen. LIST may be used in several ways.

LIST -5Ø will LIST all commands from the beginning of the program through line 5Ø.

LIST 5Ø- will LIST from line 5Ø to the end of the program.

LIST 5Ø-1ØØ will LIST all commands from line 5Ø to line 1ØØ.

LOAD This command tells the computer to place a certain named program into its memory. This command automatically erases any other program already in memory.

Missing Command Error—This means you left out a command. See Syntax Error and Chapter 4.

NEW This command tells the computer to clear its memory. It is the first step in writing a program to be sure the memory is empty.

PAUSE= This command tells the computer to wait for a certain amount of time before doing the next command. Example FOR PAUSE=1 to 15ØØ:NEXT PAUSE

PLOT _____ , _____ This command tells the computer to turn on one light on the screen. The first blank tells the computer how far over. The second blank tells the computer how far to go down.

PRINT This command tells the computer to print something on the screen. Whatever is to be printed must be inside quotation marks (" "). See Chapter 1

PRINT D $" RUN........" This command is used to tie programs together. It tells the computer to go to the diskette, find a program and RUN it.

Programs A program is a series of commands with line numbers. Commands tell the computer what to do. The line numbers tell the computer in what order to do the commands.

REM This command tells the computer to ignore the words which follow. REM stands for remark. Remarks remind us what our commands do in certain sections of the program.

RUN This command tells the computer to RUN the program in the computer's memory. To RUN a program from the diskette, type RUN followed by the name of the program you want to see.

SAVE This command will make the computer store a program. SAVE must be used with a program name. Example—SAVE apple, SAVE boat, SAVE totem.

Screen Wipe Screen wipes are a fancy way to change the screen during a program or during a graphics slide show. Screen wipes are easy to do with Variables. See Chapter 7 for examples.

PEEK(-16336) This command tells the computer to look at a certain part of its memory. When it does, the speaker clicks. More than one PEEK(-16336) command on a line will make different sounds. See Chapter 7 for sound.

STEP This command changes the way numbers are counted in FOR-NEXT commands. Example—STEP 2 tells the computer to add 2 to set the next number to be used. STEP -2 tells the computer to subtract 2 to set the next number to be used.

Syntax Error SYNTAX ERRORS are made for several reasons.
Leaving out commas in PLOT,VLIN, and HLIN commands.
Leaving out letters in a command or spelling commands with the wrong letters.

Leaving out commands when programming. I call it the "missing command" error.
Other SYNTAX ERRORS can be made by leaving out the NEXT command in the FOR-NEXT commands.

TEXT This command removes graphics from monitor's screen. Monitor then shows words on the screen rather than graphics. This is called the TEXT screen.

Variable X and Y and all letters that stand for a range of number values are called variables. Example—FOR X=∅ to 39 or FOR Y= 18 to 34. Variables can be used to save typing time.

Vertical Counters Vertical counters number the vertical columns. Vertical counters are used to measure the lengths of horizontal lines in low resolution graphics.

VLIN _____,_____ **AT** _____ This command tells the computer to draw a vertical line from one point to another at a certain column.

Index

Index